Cambridge Elements ≡

Elements in Business Strategy
edited by
J.-C. Spender
Kozminski University

GLOBAL STRATEGY IN OUR AGE OF CHAOS

How Will the Multinational Firm Survive?

Stephen B. Tallman
University of Richmond

Mitchell P. Koza
Rutgers University

CAMBRIDGE
UNIVERSITY PRESS

Shaftesbury Road, Cambridge CB2 8EA, United Kingdom

One Liberty Plaza, 20th Floor, New York, NY 10006, USA

477 Williamstown Road, Port Melbourne, VIC 3207, Australia

314–321, 3rd Floor, Plot 3, Splendor Forum, Jasola District Centre, New Delhi – 110025, India

103 Penang Road, #05–06/07, Visioncrest Commercial, Singapore 238467

Cambridge University Press is part of Cambridge University Press & Assessment, a department of the University of Cambridge.

We share the University's mission to contribute to society through the pursuit of education, learning and research at the highest international levels of excellence.

www.cambridge.org
Information on this title: www.cambridge.org/9781009500531

DOI: 10.1017/9781009384957

© Stephen B. Tallman and Mitchell P. Koza 2024

First published 2024

A catalogue record for this publication is available from the British Library.

ISBN 978-1-009-50053-1 Hardback
ISBN 978-1-009-38493-3 Paperback
ISSN 2515-0693 (online)
ISSN 2515-0685 (print)

Global Strategy in Our Age of Chaos

How Will the Multinational Firm Survive?

Elements in Business Strategy

DOI: 10.1017/9781009384957
First published online: March 2024

Stephen B. Tallman
University of Richmond

Mitchell P. Koza
Rutgers University

Author for correspondence: Stephen B. Tallman, stallman@richmond.edu

Abstract: Chaotic environments are producing unique and unprecedented challenges for multinational companies, challenges that raise important questions about whether and how multinationals will survive or wither away. This Element explores both the macro political, economic, technological, and social forces impacting international business and the strategic management adaptations that leading companies have deployed to respond to these challenges. We observe that a new organizational form – the Global Multi-Business – has evolved that may be especially adapted to respond to and challenge a world in which change is ubiquitous, with the direction of change unpredictable and the pace of change accelerating. It accomplishes this through the *strategic assembly* of the organization and the *animation* of its many parts.

Keywords: multinational management, global business, global strategy, global business environment, global supply chains

ISBNs: 9781009500531 (HB), 9781009384933 (PB), 9781009384957 (OC)
ISSNs: 2515-0693 (online), 2515-0685 (print)

Contents

1 Foreword

The withering away of the multinational firm has long been predicted. Threats from many sources have been said to herald the end of multinational firms by making them obsolete, archaic, ineffective, or inefficient (or all the aforementioned). Governments, as partners, regulators, or competitors; macroeconomics factors such as inflation, cross national regulation and control; technology, including but not limited to, dramatic increases in digital and network communications; growth and decline of product and geographic markets and market segments regionally and globally; and social movements unfriendly to multinational enterprises (MNEs) are just some of the formidable obstacles facing multinational firms (MNFs) that are thought to foreshadow demise. Yet, our personal and professional experience and our research conducted over four decades on MNFs from across the many regions of the world have left us with the inescapable conclusion that the multinational firm, as an approach to managing business across multiple national borders, is as healthy and strong today as it has ever been. At the present time, the latest accurate estimate is that there are some 60,000 MNCs worldwide, controlling more than 500,000 subsidiaries (Science Po, 2018). Of course, the multinational continues to face remarkable challenges which raise important questions for managers, investors, students of multinational business, and scholars interested in these phenomena, questions this Element will elaborate and address.

Our ambition in writing this Element for Cambridge University Press is to set aside the sky-is-falling view that the end of the age of the multinational is nigh and to address a more fundamental question; how will the multinational survive and what form of adaptation is it likely to take? Our view is coevolutionary (Koza and Lewin, 1998; Lewin and Volberda, 1999), we examine the complex dynamic between the various elements of the environments of multinational business and the adaptive responses of the MNFs themselves, as they have evolved together, mutually interacting and, at times, each affecting the other. This is the terrain for our analysis and is, in part, our motivation for writing this Element.

The narrative opens with a wide-ranging discussion of the historical environmental challenges facing multinational business from a political, economic, technological, and geographical point of view. We explore each of these separately as well as the complex interrelationships among these factors, emphasizing the importance of both the direction and the pace of change of these forces for business. We then turn to the adaptive responses of multinational business over the last century, noting the multiple transformations and logics of responses of the companies, with emphasis on the various managerial responses from leading multinational players. We provide illustrations of these processes from in-depth explorations of several companies, including, but not limited to, Nexia International, a major player in the mid-market accounting business, and Group Renault and its partners in the Turkish market for automobiles. We then return to emerging environmental challenges that derive from both major political and economic processes as well as the companies' behaviors themselves. We conclude this Element with a discussion of both the strategic imperatives driving companies' responses and our own view of both the what-is-coming and what-is-to-be-done questions, Of course, past performance is no guarantee of future adaptation so we will endeavor to gaze into our ivory tower crystal ball and look out to a future only partially foreseeable. In this, we ask the reader to test their own experience with our prognostications. Thus, we and our readers together may also, at least conceptually, coevolve.

In formulating our views, many individuals and organizations have assisted us in formulating and refining our approach. Our home institutions, including the University of Richmond, Rutgers University, INSEAD, Cranfield School of Management and UCLA, as well as the many companies which have provided us with unprecedented access deserve special notice. Our students, whether they be undergraduates, masters, doctoral candidates, or the many executives and managers we have worked with in executive education programs, have been a remarkably agile and helpful group of informants, co-conspirators, critics, and friends. Collectively, they have provided guidance and insight. Several colleagues have provided helpful comments on drafts of this manuscript, including Cambridge Elements Editor JC Spender, Oded Shenkar, Kenan Guler, and two anonymous referees. Our families have offered immense support that only individuals who have engaged in book writing can fully appreciate and understand. The Acknowledgements in the back of this Element can only partially repay their unselfish support. All of the aforementioned deserve a *grande merci*. Of course, none of these individuals or organizations have any responsibility for anything contained in these pages. Nor is it meant to represent their own points of view. We take full responsibility and at least part of the blame for what is written herein.

2 The Challenge

The global business environment is in a muddle (Tallman and Koza, 2024). The sudden onset of the coronavirus pandemic in 2020 brought the world economy to a virtual halt in the face of medical and health challenges not seen since the Spanish flu of 1918. The onslaught of the Russian army into Ukraine in 2022 caught gradually recovering global supply chains by surprise and shut down important inputs of oil, natural gas, wheat, nickel, aluminum, and other key minerals. These recent events come on top of disruptions to the global economic system created by the Trump administration's war on trade, the Biden administration's continuation and divergence from certain of those trade policies, and evolving investment with China and Europe. Moreover, the earthquake/tsunami/nuclear disasters in Japan, floods in Thailand, war in and refugee floods from Syria, and a variety of other disasters both natural and man-made have produced significant environmental shocks. And then there are the truly unprecedented existential threats of climate change, exploding population growth and aging, environmental degradation and global warming, species extinction, and food supply disruptions. The neoliberal economic policies of globalization, efficient operations, and effective information processing that have been the foundation of an expanding global economy through decades of a relatively stable world business environment are insufficient to stand up to the turbulence that has descended on global markets (Petricevic and Teece, 2019).

At the same time, and at least in part due to this turbulence, the rise of nationalism, authoritarianism, and preferences for local ownership, production, and distribution have become ascendant in Eastern and Central Europe, Turkey, India, Middle East, and Latin America – and even among a growing number of American and Western European policymakers. This is only likely to accelerate as increasingly authoritarian and xenophobic populist governments respond to pandemics, massive population shifts, income inequalities, and extensive job restructuring with isolationist economic and social policies. For instance, China's "zero COVID" policy of shutting down cities and facilities immediately and extensively upon the discovery of even a single case of the disease kept the pressure on global supply chains and contributed to accelerating inflation in much of the world. It is also widely seen as a way for the central government to justify increased surveillance and control of the population (Zero options, 2022). And, in an even more recent development, it appears that China's sudden and unexpected abandonment of the zero COVID policy is equally likely to continue disruption of global business, as vast numbers of Chinese become sick. These increased frictions in the system threaten the macro political economy and the flows of trade, capital, and investment that support multinational business on an institutional level.

Taken together, these phenomena create critical strategic and organizational challenges for multinational companies as they seek to (1) adjust to a new and less friendly environment for global business strategies and approaches, and (2) dominate in the increasingly cutthroat competition of global business.

> How can MNFs continue to deliver on heritage businesses while also exploring for new opportunities in both the product and geographic markets and market segments?

What managerial capabilities are most necessary for success, and how can they be nurtured, transferred, and protected?

How can managers defend firm-level advantages in the face of increasingly hostile and aggressive competitors, in some cases utilizing the support and resources of home country governments?

What organizational forms and strategic management approaches are most likely to predominate in the new more complex and less predictable global environment, and on what basis will they succeed and become sustainable?

Will the multinational, as we know it, survive through successful adaptation and innovation or will it be replaced by newer, better adapted, forms of economic activity and on what basis will they emerge and succeed?

Global business strategy is strategy in context. It studies "cross-border activities of economic agents or the strategies and governance of firms engaged in such activity" (Tallman and Pedersen, 2015: 273). Consequently, while all business strategy must adapt to new exogenous conditions or die, this imperative is more apparent, more immediate, and more consequential in global markets and among global multinational firms (MNFs), where crossing borders is a constant activity and organizational and environmental complexity is maximized. Strategic and organizational responses to the turbulent "new world order" are essential for companies hoping to be "selected in," to borrow Darwinian terminology. How can companies deliver on demands for sustainability, adaptability, and local identity while also providing for worldwide reach, world-class technology, and world-beating competitiveness? What can we expect of tomorrow's companies as they adapt to the newly turbulent world order and try to manage these cross pressures? And how do the short and long terms compare as MNFs contemplate major, "bet the company" redirection and investment while industries seem to move to "winner take all" outcomes? Can slack-ridden "just in case" operational and logistical strategies really drive out low-cost, efficient "just in time" and "just enough" strategies in the face of global financial market pressures – which themselves are likely to be exacerbated, not mitigated, by this same turbulent, more uncertain, higher risk global order? These are the related questions and issues that we will address, and seek to provide an answer, in this Element. Our work and approach is based on over four decades of research in international and global business and includes studies of multinational companies in countries across the globe.

The End of a Liberal World Order?

Well before the world slipped into its current macro-turbulence – geopolitical, environmental, cultural, demographic, health, cultural – we were observing trends away from the traditional large, vertically integrated, bureaucratic multinational company as the mainstay of the international economy. Indeed, we were seeing trends away from the post–World War II political and economic liberal world order, driven by assumptions of the ultimate superiority of democratic political structures and market economics. Of course, the Cold War between the liberal democracies of the West and the command economies of totalitarian socialist powers in the Soviet Union and China and their satellite nations offered a challenge, and the "Third World" was too poor to contribute much but primary commodity products to world markets. Global strategy took these nations into account, but primarily as input providers and markets for generic products from the technologically advanced market economies, provided by MNFs based in the "Industrial Triad" nations of North America, Western Europe, and Japan (Rugman, 2005). Market forces driven by innovation, capital, and market power offered seductions to the people behind the Iron Curtain and opportunities to the masses in "the global South" that would eventually pull them into the liberal market world. Indeed, with the fall of the Berlin Wall and the dissolution of the Soviet Union, Fukuyama (1992) famously declared the victory of Western liberal democracy and "the end of history," just as the forces that subsequently undermined the liberal world order and the Western industrial nation-based multinationals that have been its main agents were being set loose. So much for the end of history!

These forces are technological, sociopolitical, and economic in nature. They have in large part been created or at least promulgated and nurtured by the very MNFs that they have now come to threaten. Perhaps the single most important factor driving and permitting change was the information and communication technology (ICT) revolution initiated with the invention of the transistor at Bell Labs in 1947, just after World War II, and the subsequent development of semiconductor chips, microprocessors, business and personal computers, software such as UNIX, and the like. Increased computing power, increased transmission bandwidth, increasingly small devices, increasingly powerful software, and increasingly sophisticated users recalibrated transactional relationships in global markets. Increasing efficiency no longer required tight bureaucratic controls when vast arrays of data were available and easily analyzed in close to real time.

At the same time, countries that had been kept out of the main global market economy began to engage at a new level of ambition and capability. Politically, the fall of the Soviet Union and emergence of Eastern Europe matched with the opening of China under Deng Xiaoping to add a billion and a half (more or less) new market participants to the global economy, organized into nations that were too large and potentially powerful to be ignored. The 1990s also saw economic growth and development and political liberalization in the Americas, Africa, the Middle East, and South Asia. The communist "Second World" set aside the Iron

Curtain, while the "Third World" reached the political and economic point where many of its countries could no longer be relegated to being simple primary product sources. As these countries began to push against the post war industrial market economies, they emerged as new markets and production sites for technologically advanced products and their own multinational firms became serious competitors to the traditionally dominant multinationals. The dominance and hegemony of North American– and Western European–based companies faced unprecedented and sustained challenges from the growing and prospering upstart "newcomers."

Information and Communication Technology

While the impact of ICT is far from complete, certain trends that are dependent on technology have become apparent since the dawn of the twenty-first century. Supply chains have become longer and more complex, and increasingly dependent on outsourcing specialists in distant locations. "Factoryless goods producers" like Apple or Nike own few productive (in the traditional sense) assets but control their global value chains (GVCs) and accumulate most of the network profits by tightly controlling critical intangible assets (Buckley et al., 2022). Only the increasing use of ICT made possible the radical offshoring and outsourcing that we have seen leading up to (and amplifying, if not creating) the current crises. Downstream value propositions have also undergone deep structural change. This can be seen clearly when services, such as ride sharing from Uber and Lyft, hourly leases from Toro, or scooters from Lime and Bird, replace ownership of cars and motorcycles for personal transportation. In manufacturing we have seen similar, if at times surprising, innovations; Tesla manages complex supplier and component manufacturing contractor relations upstream, but turning the services approach on its head sells cars directly to consumers, disintermediating traditional dealer/manufacturing arrangements, suggesting there may be some life left in the traditional vertical integration approach along some elements of the value chain. Thus, the rise of the "gig economy" and other approaches to radically decentralized value delivery to customers substituted ICT for bureaucratic oversight and allowed firms to maintain tight control over armies of "contractors" while managing resource expenditures and exposure in international markets.

ICT was both a major facilitator of globalization for the world economy and a major driver as an industry, or industries. To begin with the latter case, it is apparent that hardware production for ICT is the epitome of global sourcing. The Apple iPhone, as has been often described, is assembled in Southern China by a Taiwanese firm using components sourced from the USA, South Korea,

Southeast Asia, and China, among other countries. The majority of integrated circuit chips for the world are fabricated in Taiwan, South Korea, and China. Even when assembled in the USA or Europe, most electronic (and electronics-dependent) goods are made of components sourced from around the world, but most notably from China. Much software still originates in the USA and other developed countries, but much of the actual code writing and debugging is done in India or other emerging markets. The "production value smile" (Mudambi, 2008), which shows that high value creativity and innovation and high value sales and marketing are focused in developed economies while lower value manufacturing and assembly tend to be assigned to emerging markets, remains in place – but has weakened as China and other emerging markets have themselves become innovators and major markets. As we shall see, though, it may end as a grim horizontal line on the face of the current chaotic political-economic conditions.

ICT has also facilitated the globalization of supply and markets by eliminating many of the uncertainties driven by limited communication among widely spread value-adding sites, headquarters, and customers in all industries. Building components in China, tracking them in shipping containers around the world, landing them in developed countries, and having them arrive on schedule as part of a global "just in time" supply chain require significant ICT support. Writing code on a twenty-four-hour cycle that rotates between India and the USA requires seamless communication and powerful computing. Directing and redirecting oil tankers in mid-ocean requires satellite monitoring, constantly updated market analysis, and instant communication. For that matter, the need for vast and sophisticated ICT by fast fashion phenomena such as Shein of China, involving sourcing fabrics, outsourcing production, assembling information on demand patterns, and advertising through TikTok and other electronic media is breathtaking (in ways both good and bad). As a consequence, some have observed that company headquarters today is becoming less to do with geographic location and more to do with managing a consensus regarding corporate mission, values, and norms. The command-and-control approach of the traditional vertically integrated bureaucratic firms, tightly managed from the HQ, appears insufficiently able to provide the requisite "control," requiring innovative solutions. (Tallman and Koza, 2010).

Rise of the Emerging Market Countries

As more and more countries moved from relatively low levels of development into "emerging market economy" status, MNEs looked to them (and especially the Big Emerging Markets [BEMs] of China, India, Brazil, South Africa, Nigeria, and the like) as large and potentially rapidly growing markets and, critically, as low-cost sources of production for themselves and for the developed world. The role of putative "Second and Third World" countries – now typically categorized as emerging markets when they have the level of sophistication, education, and infrastructure to supply the world ICT market – is no longer peripheral and focused on low-value products. Companies in these countries and in other nascent industrial economies have become more sophisticated and more integrated into the world economy as the countries offered better educated and trained workers and their own intangible assets. As a result, the possibilities for MNEs to outsource non-core – but not unimportant – activities to these countries, or for emerging market firms to extend their operations into developed markets, seemingly became endless. This information-age approach to business, whether dispersed manufacturing or remotely owned personal services delivered by "independent contractors," builds the global organization around the "one big idea," a brand, a few lines of code, and a minimum of recognized full-time employees. This increasingly dispersed, market-based, and ICT-driven globalization of markets and supply chains was typified by the rise of China as an essential market, the vital source in many global supply chains, and increasingly as the homebase of many rapidly expanding and highly competitive MNFs of its own. Even the 2008 global recession had at best a temporary impact on this system, which only gathered itself for further expansion using the same model within a couple of years.

The rise of offshore manufacturing was highlighted by opposition to the North American Free Trade Agreement (NAFTA), seen as opening the door to moving low-cost production out of the United States, but with the United States remaining the primary market. By the time of the 2004 American presidential election, recognition arose that China was the actual beneficiary of much of this offshoring and moreover that many business services were also moving offshore, often to India (Blinder, 2006). At the same time, largely domestic firms were looking to outsource their international production rather than trying to manage factories or call centers in emerging markets, and developing ICT made monitoring contract performance more reliable and less expensive. Emerging market countries, with large, increasingly educated and trained, newly urbanized work forces offered low-cost, efficient, and reliable production for the global logistical system as well as seemingly insatiable demand for the products of the same MNFs. The wealth deriving from industrialization and urbanization drove rapid expansion of consumer demand in emerging markets, providing increasing economies of scale and scope and more than doubling the worldwide customer bases for their products.

The Rise of Free Trade and the Globalization of Markets

Concurrently with the emergence of these big new markets, driven by the demands of workers and customers worldwide, and enabled by increasingly powerful ICT, the world's system of foreign trade and investment expanded dramatically. The creation and growth of the World Trade Organization and the inclusion of EM countries such as China in the WTO system of ever-freer trade and investment that characterized the neoliberal world led to the rapid globalization of markets. Falling tariffs and disappearing investment limitations characterized both EM and industrialized market countries. The opening of the very large emerging market countries like India and China and the collapse of the Soviet Union in the late 1980s and early 1990s were particularly notable in the trend toward globalization.

Multinational firms from the industrial West sought access to these massive economies as visions of incredible growth and profitability danced in their heads. As MNFs gained access, they discovered that these countries could provide inexpensive labor to produce even complex products and to deliver highly technical services for much less money. Thus, a major story during the last thirty years of the global liberal economy has been the offshoring of mass production, first of standard components, but increasingly of final goods, to China and other emerging markets, with the concomitant growth of global logistics systems and trade in both intermediate and final goods. Ever-freer trade, a rules-based world order, and densely integrated networks allowed efficiency to rule in "the global factory" (Buckley and Strange, 2011) as uncertainty seemed to disappear. Worldwide just-in-time supply chains produced globalized products based on universal technologies to satisfy increasingly convergent demand across markets in all places and at all levels of development. Value was delivered by innovation, technology, branding, and integration, no longer by tightly controlled, vertically integrated manufacturing.

As pointed out earlier, emerging market countries worked not only as efficient sources of goods and services, but increasingly became markets for the technologies, brands, goods, and services generated in the industrial world. As China became the world's second largest economy, its increasingly skilled and better-paid workers and a burgeoning entrepreneurial class provided massive new demand for goods and services produced both domestically and internationally, by local companies and the largest MNFs from around the world. Likewise, India, Brazil, Russia, and many smaller emerging markets began demanding access to world-class goods and services even as they grew by acting as sources for goods in the Western world.

The global trading system of the first decades of the twenty-first century offered a vision of efficiency-driven capitalism on a global scale. Originally, foreign direct investment was seen as allowing firms to produce goods in their final market instead of exporting large, expensive final products from the home country – replacing trade. Over time, though, firms rationalized production on a regional and worldwide basis, trade barriers and investment came down, the use of shipping containers became ubiquitous, and ICT made global coordination and international oversight feasible – trade increased, though much more of it was in intermediate goods. Industry leader Caterpillar, the Peoria, Illinois-based, manufacturer of earth moving equipment, pioneered this approach, centralizing capital-intensive scale-driven manufacturing of major components such as engines, transmissions, and axles at home, while localizing assembly and add-on design and manufacturing to dealers in the local markets.

Technology, redundancy, and integration in the global factory created flexible, responsive, decentralized networks of supply and distribution that were expected to be robust to disruptions in one part of the system as other providers covered for them (Buckley and Ghauri, 2004). The drive for economic efficiency, growth in markets, and short-term profitability together at a time of few constraints seemed likely to end in a globalized market for most goods and indeed for many services – especially those involving information processing and transmission.

Economic pressures and falling barriers led MNFs not just to offshore locations, but to offshore production specialists, and as leading firms began to use offshore production, cost pressures drove their competitors to do the same. Where a few decades earlier, MNFs felt that direct control through ownership of international production was critical for cross-border production networks, increasingly efficient logistics and ever-better ICT allowed firms to turn the relatively low-value and often labor-intensive actual production of things over to local partners. Apple, Nike, or Uniqlo could focus on innovation, technology, design, and marketing – the sources of real value – and let local manufacturers deal with local workers and governments (Mudambi, 2008). While global logistics networks grew, the MNFs at their centers often reduced their internal presence in foreign countries, using long-lasting contracts and minority ties to hand the messy work of making things over to reliable suppliers. The central MNF became a network orchestrator as well as a technology and marketing innovator.

3 The Multinational as an Adaptive Organization: From the Multinational to the Transnational to the Global Multi-Business

The complexity and unpredictability of these many trends produced waves of innovation in MNF management and organization and, along with it, a significant stream of research on these issues. Table 1 provides an overview

Table 1 The evolution of multinational business

Growth logic	Diversification	Leveraging competencies	Strategic assembly
Managerial task	Capital allocation	Interdivisional cooperation	Balancing exploitation & exploration
Control mechanism	Financial controls	Behavior controls	Enabling emergent process
Leadership	Command and control	Coaching	Animation

* Adapted from Koza and Lewin, 1996 and Tallman and Koza, 2010.

of this research and summarizes the evolution of approaches to multinational management over the last three quarters of a century. The table contrasts three distinct models from multinational management theory and practice.

First, we identify the Multinational approach, with its emphasis on financial controls and unrelated diversification, followed by the transnational solution to challenges with the first model, most importantly underexploited opportunities for cross-unit cooperation. Most recently, and central to our understanding of the direction that multinationals are moving, is the third approach, the Global Multi-Business, an approach uniquely adapted to chaotic environments. While there are significant differences within each of these three models separately, the differences between and among these models are most significant and capture major trends in multinational management. Figure 1 illustrates relevant organizational differences among these models. Next, we elaborate each model with respect to important elements of organizational morphology and process, with special emphasis on the nascent Global Multi-Business model. These include, but are not limited to, growth, key management challenges, control mechanisms, and leadership styles. By recognizing these stages as typically, although not exclusively, an evolutionary process, it is possible to understand each approach as a solution, in some respects, to challenges emergent in prior stages. It is suggestive of the rationale for the persistence and potential inertia of prior stages as newer ones emerge.

The Multinational

The modern multinational is a remarkably new phenomenon. Although we have evidence of international business over 4,000 years ago, with the flourishing trade between the Indus Valley city of Harappa and Ur, the modern-day

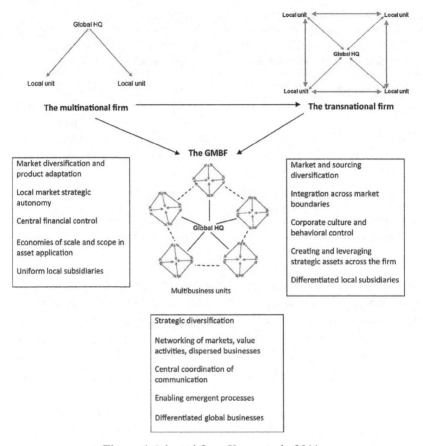

Figure 1 Adapted from Koza, et al., 2011

multinational primarily grew out of the economic expansion in the post–World War II period of the late 1940s to the 1960s. There is some evidence of multinationals, such as the Dutch-Anglo company Unilever or Royal Dutch Shell, that emerged in the period prior to the war, and indeed, the common stock companies of the eighteenth and nineteenth centuries predate those, but the multinational as we know it is a largely postwar phenomenon, primarily dominated by companies based in North America and Western Europe.

Led by Harold Geneen, perhaps the most illustrious of the era's CEOs, International Telephone and Telegraph (ITT) is arguably the prototypical example of the multinational approach. With its strong ambition for diversification through acquisitions – some 350 acquisitions in 80 countries, focus on capital allocation from the corporate headquarters, reliance on financial controls and a leadership style based on finance-based command and control from the center, ITT successfully managed several hundred separate divisionalized and often unrelated companies and profit centers at various times in its heyday. Indeed, it was so successful that the company became identified as an incubator for chief executive officers, seeding the "C Suites" of several other companies. This can be thought of as the "age of the conglomerate." However, with the increasing integration of the world economic order as the post–Bretton Woods regime took hold, the emergence and recognition of the conglomerate discount by the academic and financial community, that is, the reduction in value assessed by the market due to unrelated businesses grouped together under one organizational umbrella, and its insistence on relatedness as a justification for diversification (Rumelt, 1974) into new businesses and business segments, and ever-greater competitive pressures for efficiency and innovation, multinationals such as ITT faced enormous pressures for a different and more competitive approach to international operations. Conglomerates, with few notable exceptions, as a business approach faced being "selected out" by competitive and market forces.

The Transnational

The transnational emerged, in part, as a response to these challenges of political and economic integration and calls for relatedness faced by multinationals. With its focus on core competencies and the imperative to leverage competencies though interdivisional cooperation, emphasis on behavior controls to complement financial controls, and coaching as a leadership style, the transnational prospered in the period of the latter twentieth century (cf. Bartlett and Ghoshal, 1989). Exemplars of the transnational approach include, among many others, Asea Brown Boveri (ABB), led by Percy Barnevik, Procter and Gamble, especially in its consumer products areas, Saatchi and Saatchi, and Honda, with its diversification into power packs, lawnmowers, and snowblowers to complement its heritage activities in motorcycles and automobiles. These companies responded to the imperative of realizing the benefits of intraorganizational cooperation across business units to achieve some form of value-adding activity, and thus sought to justify integrating disparate activities within the company, through both vertical and horizontal integration utilizing competencies as a basis for diversification. At Honda, for instance, competency was based on the ability to adapt small engines to a variety of uses, at Sony it was miniaturization, and at Proctor and Gamble the ability to manage the branding process. The challenges of transforming companies from the multinational approach to the transnational dominated teaching, research, and theorizing in strategic management departments of business schools during much of this period.

However, limits to the transnational as a solution to the challenges of multinational management became increasingly obvious to managers, investors, observers, and academics as the twenty-first century dawned and both the direction and the pace of change became increasingly unpredictable. Additionally, the concept of "core competence," a powerful and useful construct as originally conceived (Prahalad and Hamel, 1985), was stretched to the point where managers were claiming human resources, engineering, finance, and the full range of traditional business functions as both "core" and "competences." Clearly, at least some transnational pioneers risked becoming stretched beyond their elastic limits. Transnationals confronted the risk of differentiating across disparate markets, businesses, segments, products, and so on without the "glue" of managerial capability to provide sufficient integration of these critical functions and radically differentiated operations and businesses. Some critics observed that the risk of conglomerates, like the once-lauded Hanson Trust, a subsidiary of the German company Heidelberg Cement, and delisted from the London Stock Exchange since August 2007, could once again become ascendant.

The Rise of the Global Multi-Business

In a system where global integration of national markets was increasing year on year, as were information technology–based control mechanisms, with armies of increasingly skilled workers available across the many emerging market countries, something new was needed. With its focus on innovation everywhere, lean organization, and growth incentives, the network organization, made up of many suppliers bound to a "flagship" global MNF (Rugman and D'Cruz, 1997) by common interests, economic incentives, and information systems as opposed to bureaucratic rules or common ownership, seemed an increasingly apparent answer. The partial dissolution of large, bureaucratic, and vertically integrated MNFs in favor of dispersed networks of value-adding firms focused on innovation, flexibility, and responsiveness seemed a rational response to the demands of a rapidly developing world and increasingly powerful information technology with its potential for greatly expanded ability of firms to manage complexity (Tallman and Koza, 2010, 2016).

The Global Multi-Business Firm (GMBF) approach, the most recent approach to multinational business (Tallman and Koza, 2010; Koza et al., 2011), promises to respond to, and/or manage, these risks. Its primary contribution is to describe a twofold model of strategic organization and oversight (control being too strong a word for the loose guidance that is key to the concept). Ideally, these global lead firms cut headcount, capital investment, and actual internal production to the bone, replacing commitment with flexibility, bureaucracy with technology, tangibles with intangibles. Firms became MNFs by moving production to countries that had become major markets and then using these sites also to supply the original home market and other international locations, as described years earlier in Vernon's (1966) International Product Life Cycle model, but still through intra-firm trade – exports kept within the boundaries of the firm (Casson, 1987). The rapid evolution of global markets and the accession of large emerging market countries, especially China, into the World Trade Organization allowed firms to consider widespread offshore production, possibly, but not necessarily, servicing the producing nation, but primarily aimed at a worldwide market.

Understanding the Promise of Global Multi-Business Firms

The GMBF concept draws from earlier proposals for decentralized and dispersed, but also strategically responsive and adaptive organizations (cf. Koza and Lewin, 1996). Zenger and Hesterly (1997) offer principles for information-age organizations of radical decentralization, unit autonomy, and strong-form market controls, whether a unit is internal to the central corporation or not. Rewards are based on unit outputs, with further incentives for cooperation and joint innovation. Similarly, McDermott et al. (2013) describe global modular production systems in which global activities are partitioned into functionally and geographically isolated units, with the parent MNF providing an architecture for managing inputs and outputs, while leaving the modules (whether in-house or outsourced) to manage internal operations autonomously. The GMBF approach further develops the idea of a globally networked organization with widely dispersed value-adding units with highly autonomous decision-making and frequently without ownership ties to the central MNF. It also considers how to use market-like reward structures to incentivize operational cooperation and strategic integration, while providing levels of coordination and communication that make pursuing common goals the preferred strategy. The age-old challenge of producing cooperation through voluntary effort (cf. Barnard, 1938) was, once again, central to the management of these firms.

The Concept

Tallman and Koza (2010) proposed the GMBF as a unique and uniquely capable model to describe business organizations for the global information-age economy. Their GMBF offers a solution to the problem of encouraging both production efficiency and constant innovation across many national markets and value-production sites without becoming enmeshed in bureaucratic controls on a global scale or losing a sense of strategic leadership for the GMBF as a whole. Traditional approaches to the MNE also describe network organizations with increasingly powerful national subsidiaries (Bartlett and Ghoshal, 1989), tied to each other and to the central headquarters in various ways involving hierarchical control, financial oversight, and cultural understanding (Ghoshal and Nohria, 1989). These models tend to envision a central, ownership-based core, albeit one with strong informal as well as formal ties, with national subsidiaries linking to loosely tied networks of affiliates and contractors (Cantwell, 2013). Narula and Dunning (2010) took the further step of recognizing that the central core was no longer defined by common ownership. Tallman and Koza (2010) build on these ideas to describe an organization defined more by strategic intended and emergent processes than by legal boundaries.

Putting the GMBF Together

The GMBF is constructed through the process of *strategic assembly* of highly skilled organizational units, imbued with relevant capabilities and based in optimal locations. These value-adding elements are carefully accessed through the full range of governance mechanisms, including, but not limited to, joint ventures, alliances, acquisitions, greenfield investments – and contracts, sub-contracts, and informal understandings such as work sharing agreements. This "Lego-like" building block approach to corporate organization promises to achieve maximum "fit" with the strategic ambition of firms while maintaining the flexibility and agility necessary to be de-assembled when no longer needed. Flexibility is built in by minimizing capital commitment and the biases of ownership. Wholly owned subsidiaries tend to pull the global firm toward resource exploitation, strategic inertia, and the sunk cost fallacy. Strategic assembly suggests that ownership and capital investment be avoided when possible in favor of lower commitment, strong incentives for both efficiency and innovation, and the ability to switch out organizational parts on the fly.

Strategic assembly, or building the organization in a strategic manner, requires the MNF to develop a deep understanding of complex goals, competing needs for innovation, flexibility, and resilience, and strident and often conflicting demands from external stakeholders. It refers to the considered use of the full range of organization building options, including, but not limited to, internal development, mergers, acquisitions, joint ventures, syndicates, and strategic alliances to construct the formal and informal organization. Where and how to draw the permeable boundaries of modern companies is a constant and ongoing strategic discussion for senior managers, boards of directors, regulators, workers, unions, and governmental officials (Koza et al., 2011). Understanding what assets are the real basis of competitive advantage for the MNE is essential – and these are often small, but critical bits of knowledge rather than vast, expensive processing facilities. At the same time, knowing where to position or access resources – both strategic and complementary – is essential to the cost efficiency that came to drive the global system. And, finally, governance, and particularly the choice of owning assets versus accessing them as needed, provides the network with the flexibility that is needed to adjust quickly to changing demand patterns and supply variations.

The GMBF is an example of the networked organization that Zenger and Hesterly (1997) referred to as an information age disaggregated corporation. In this model, individual "molecular" units are assembled according to corporate requirements for their specific capabilities, with little regard to ownership or tight control. The GMBF is not conducive to overall central bureaucratic control, as units come and go and are expected to remain largely autonomous. Formal controls are expected to be limited to inputs and outputs within a modular value-production system, and cultural controls become problematic when the various units are both geographically dispersed and often independent outsourced suppliers. This model of the networked organization emphasizes strong assets, flexibility, and agility in the face of an uncertain environment – but must also retain strategic direction and organizational efficiency. What makes it all work?

Making the GMBF Run

This need for operational and strategic control without the ability to command or demand calls for the second key concept, *strategic animation*, to achieve the often elusive "on paper" promises of performance without the restrictions of internal control and global bureaucracy of earlier models of the MNF. Strategic animation (Koza et al., 2011; Tallman and Koza, 2016) describes the processes for providing strategic direction, incentives for both efficiency and innovation, and managerial motivation – all the while maintaining flexibility, adaptability, and responsiveness by minimizing bureaucratic oversight, sunk investment, and organizational homogeneity. In newly assembled companies it is not uncommon to lack traditional tools of rewards, measurement, and other incentives. For these companies, management without control is a new strategic imperative. By using market-like incentives, common managerial technology, modular task structures, and other tools to make cooperation efficient and rewarding, global MNFs are pioneering ways to motivate a widespread network of affiliates, subsidiaries, partners, and contractors to work cooperatively to the benefit of all through self-interest (Tallman and Koza, 2016).

Global bureaucracy, with its formal structures, command-and-control approach to governance and direction, vertical integration – and inflexibility, inability to adapt to changing context, and limited incentives for innovation for most operational units – is ill-suited to the demands of the global information economy. At the same time, simple contracts for supply, production, or distribution offer process efficiency, but at the cost of organizational stress. Together, managerial focus on assembly and animation promises to rebalance managerial action in firms, complementing the individual business units with their focus on business strategy with the increasing value from the center. Corporate strategy and business strategy must become complementary, replacing both the heavy hand of command and control and the potentially directionless compliance "coaching" within globally networked organizations (Tallman and Koza, 2016).

The premise underlying animation is that given the proper setting and incentives, processes will emerge naturally as the units of the GMBF interact and the various units will tend to self-organize without a heavy-handed bureaucracy. The goal is to encourage virtual integration of the strategically assembled organization without the "firm-level command economy" (Tallman and Koza, 2016) of the bureaucratic model. This is driven by voluntary engagement driven by economic, financial, technical, and behavioral incentives that make strategic integration and cooperation both the easiest and the most profitable direction for each unit – pursuing "the easier right."

We identify three principles found to encourage voluntary integration.

1) Facilitate strategic decision-making autonomy for the top management of each modular unit.

By allowing these managers to make choices about optimal investments in process technologies, training, scale, and so on, the central headquarters can focus on its role as system integrator, concerned with the overall product and focused on specifying inputs and outputs across the modules rather than operation control of separable activities. We see this in the examples of Apple and Nike, which moved actual manufacturing of their devices and shoes offshore and to outsourcing specialists, thus avoiding the need for direct managerial control of massive production facilities in an unfamiliar foreign setting. Of course, autonomy tends to lead to self-interest, so a second principle is needed.

2) Create and manage incentives for cooperation.

These can be both cost- and income-based. That is, the GMBF can offer communication technology, product technologies, process education, financing, and so on to make working within its system the preferred path. This is combined with strong-form market incentives for units and their managers to allow them to keep at least a part of the savings from increased efficiency (both local and system-wide) and participation in the rewards from innovation (both process and product). By treating all units, whether internal, affiliated, or contracted, as autonomous organizations with similar incentive structures, cooperation and coordination can become the preferred choice. With these incentives in place, bureaucratic direction from the central HQ must give way to alternative governance, leading to our third principle.

3) Promulgating and exploiting self-organization.

The central GMBF headquarters can focus on easing communication, putting the strategic managers of units together, creating communities of practice, and offering a vision of the future at a system-wide level. At the same time, the headquarters do not need to focus on a formal bureaucratic structure – behavioral evidence suggests that people faced with a common challenge and given a bit of incentive and opportunity will organize themselves (and their elements) to improve efficiency and effectiveness in addressing common problems. The headquarters need not establish command or control – rather, if it can smooth communication and enable coordination and reward cooperation and integration, the strategically assembled parts of the GMBF will work out ways to work together.

Applications of the Global Multi-Business

By the early 2000s, many firms were pursuing the principles of the GMBF as their supply chains moved further offshore from their key markets, their intellectual property development was dispersed to reflect regional differences in technology and demand, and outsourcing specialists from emerging market countries proved to be both competent and economical.

In Global Manufacturing: Renault and Its Turkish Partners

The spread of GVCs during the 1990s and 2000s moved many manufacturing firms in the direction of the GMBF, though largely without that intention. As discussed earlier, this era saw the emergence of many large countries onto the global economic stage both as markets and as production sites, especially for labor-intensive production. It was also the beginning of the ICT revolution, where the ability to oversee production chains closely at great distances, whether internal or contracted, became ubiquitous. Gereffi et al. (2005) recognized that GVCs were, in fact, not restricted to make or buy alternatives, but rather reflected a number of alternatives where mutual dependencies, relational ties, and bilateral investments could make networks of modular production sites stable, cost efficient, and responsive. Bair (2008) describes a Global Production

Network in which modular production (McDermott et al., 2013; Sturgeon, 2002) systems operated by outsourcing specialists are backed up by the core MNF. The headquarters specifies and manages the modular structure and key design aspects of the inputs and outputs of the various modules and creates and oversees the communication and logistics systems that connect them. However, the modular units manage their internal systems according to their own ideas.

We can see the dispersion and de-integration of supply (and distribution) chains in many manufacturing industries, and among some of the best-known multinational brands – Apple, Nike, Uniqlo, Boeing, and many others. As a more detailed example, though, we offer a case from an earlier work (Koza et al., 2011), that of Group Renault and Renault Turkey. Renault provides a good example of the transition from multinational to transnational to GMBF, as it has gradually expanded both its geographical and its organizational networks. Of course, Renault is, and has been, deeply involved with a variety of partners worldwide (most notoriously with Nissan Motors of Japan), itself a feature of the GMBF configuration, but its operations in Turkey are notable for our purposes. It has been in Turkey since 1969 in partnership with Oyak (the Armed Forces Pension Fund, which owns 49 percent of Oyak-Renault). The original purpose of the Turkish operations was to manufacture Renault cars for the Turkish market, offering cost, cultural, and regulatory advantages of imports from France. Over time, production levels increased, as did the local market, and more models were included as were exports to regional markets. Even as the Turkish organization took on an increasing role as regional strategic leader, its equity joint venture governance structure was maintained – not the usual approach of Renault, but one suited to the unique conditions of the Turkish market.

Ties between the French parent company and the Turkish joint venture are maintained and strengthened by personnel exchanges and secondments at every level. Production workers from Turkey visit plants in France. Managers from France continue to serve stints in Turkey (Koza et al. [2011] note that four French managers were resident in Turkey in 2010), but we also see substantial numbers of Turkish managers serving in France and, most notably, in third countries. These expatriate assignments serve as legitimate career boosts for both French and Turkish individuals. Top country managers in the Middle East and North Africa are sent from Turkey rather than France, Turkish engineers monitor and support plants in the region (and in Latin America), and production teams from the region receive training in Turkey rather than France. Turkey provides parts and components to the worldwide Renault logistics network directly, as opposed to being tasked by the French headquarters. Out of this evolutionary process, and in concert with other alliances and ties, Renault has become a global force in the automobile industry as a GMBF, neither surrendering its French nature at home, nor insisting on French dominance elsewhere. Indeed, Renault is by no means a dominant player in the European Union market, and without the capabilities and support offered by its deeply engaged partnerships would be an unlikely major force in the global industry.

In Global Professional Services: Nexia International

One of the most successful examples of the new globally networked multibusiness firms we have studied for over three decades is Nexia International, an accounting company with 270 member firms in 125 countries. Nexia International is itself a non-equity alliance designed to provide critical international referral opportunities for its member firms. Each member firm is selected because of its operational and professional excellence and a strategy of serving the middle market in its home country. When its business clients grow and develop international extensions to their businesses Nexia offers those clients the advantage of a specialist accounting company in its expanded market as well as a partner company of equal competence to its accountancy in its home country facilitating effective and seamless cross-border coordination. A key feature of Nexia is its substitution of successfully enabling emergent management practices in the absence of traditional managerial approaches of command and control, coaching, and the like. As a non-equity alliance, the Director of Nexia lacks the tools of traditional administration utilized in either the multinational or transnational forms. Securing voluntary compliance to the wishes of superordinates, an age-old challenge of management (cf. Barnard, 1938), is especially thorny in this context, made so by both the lack of traditional control mechanisms and the increasing necessity of balancing the need to exploit heritage businesses as well as explore for new opportunities.

A unique feature of Nexia International is its recruitment and socialization functions. Potential member firms are recruited through a strict process of identifying players with exceptional fit with the ambitions of Nexia International (candidate firms must exhibit national ambition, professional excellence, middle-market focus, desire for professional development opportunities, and personal fit) and are recruited through an extensive set of on-site interviews and discussions. Once admitted to the Nexia "club", norms and values of the company are transmitted, inculcated, and supported through a variety of governance committees, system-wide meetings and gatherings, management workshops, secondments of employees, and the like. Similar to the role of the harvest in Bordeaux and Burgundy and Clifford Geertz's famous Balinese cockfight (1972), these rituals have both an instrumental ambition of socializing new entrants and a normative purpose of providing sources of integration of individuals, both people and organizational units, into the larger organization. They complement and support the management ambition of voluntary compliance without control.

In both examples, the networked model of the GMBF offered adaptability to the realities of varied and very different markets while enabling the lead firm to provide a consistent customer experience around the world. By moving critical responsibilities to affiliates, the central headquarters avoid the problem of making strategic decisions without deep knowledge and understanding, but by offering an incentive-based animation approach, they are also able to guide the decentralized network in a truly strategic manner. Of course, both firms built their GMBF models in the fairly stable environment of the late twentieth century.

4 The Critical Challenges: The World Changes and the System Turns Chaotic

And then, the environment changed dramatically, producing unique and unprecedented strategic management challenges. Following a relatively brief stable period for MNFs in the late twentieth and early twenty-first centuries, both the pace and direction of change in the global business environment became increasingly unpredictable. The sudden onset of viruses, both real and virtual, wars, using both trade policies and guns, of labor strife and populism, isolationism, and political disintegration has generated a business environment that is highly sensitive to unexpected variations in inputs. A bat bites a vendor in a Chinese "wet market", a research lab has a leak, and the global economy faces potential collapse while millions of people become ill and many die. Germans cannot import oil from Russia to run their automobiles, and Americans in Los Angeles find that prices on their previously widely available gasoline stocks go through the roof. Ukraine's farm output is bottled up in the port of Odessa by the Russian navy, and people go hungry in Africa and bread prices escalate in Portland, Oregon. Authoritarian rulers of one country after another blame and scapegoat immigrants, racial groups, minority religions, and democracy, and utilize exports as weapons, threatening investment, reductions in labor supplies, and, in the case of Russia and Ukraine, fight wars (Tallman and Koza, 2024).

These new realities are changing power relationships between MNFs and their global value chain partners and between MNFs and the governments where they operate (Buckley et al, 2022). Fragmentation of production of goods has stalled while royalties and license fees in services have grown faster than foreign direct investment and trade since 2010 (Buckley et al., 2022). The supposed resilience of the global system has been undermined by the drive for efficiency and low costs.

The entire network of international trade and investment risks failing to deliver on its promises and may well be teetering on the brink of collapse. Global supply networks were struggling in early 2020 as a result of Brexit in Europe and the Trump tariffs on steel and aluminum and on many other Chinese goods, plus expected retaliation from China, the European Union, and other countries. The onset of the COVID-19 pandemic at that time simply shut down global supply networks as China closed production in many cities, ports there stopped loading, ports in the United States and other importers stopped unloading, trucks, trains, and airplanes stopped moving goods and people, and fear gripped much of the world. Workers in retail, transportation, hospitality, and other personal service industries were laid off or stayed home – or got sick. A great part of world commerce stopped for a short time and resumed in a halting and inconsistent fashion for a year.

By late in 2022, people and companies started to resume their lives, due partly to the approval and diffusion of mRNA-based vaccines. Consequently, overstressed supply lines collapsed, goods like semiconductor chips became unavailable, slowing the production of finished automobiles, prices jumped, and a feared global economic collapse suddenly gave way to record inflation across much of the world. Pent-up demand ran into defunded supply. And as this condition began to finally ease, Russia invaded Ukraine with military force, justifying this aggression with of claims of correcting alleged historical wrongs. Subsequently, supply disruptions of Ukrainian grain and minerals and sanctions on Russian exports followed, leaving the world with a shortage of wheat and other essential foods, oil and natural gas, and essential minerals and rare earths – all industries that relied in great part on commodity production in Ukraine, Russia, or both. European need for petrochemical products to replace those flowing from Russia produced strains between the United States and key European countries. And increased food, energy, and transportation costs, economic sanctions, increased suspicion of immigrants, and fears of the political and medical risks of travel and tourism led quickly to a further burst of inflation across the world, and significant struggles for even the most modern globally networked and resourced MNEs.

The Systemic Challenges

These macro political and economic dislocations have had substantial effects on business policy, some predictable, others unforeseeable, raising challenging conundrums for managers. What are the key specific challenges, natural and man-made, that have developed to create the chaotic system for business that has become apparent in the last decade? How can the GMBF affectively respond to these challenges and what will those adaptations likely look like? On what basis can MNEs successfully compete in the new environment? We have identified four key related classes of challenges and their corresponding implications for managers of MNEs: politics and policies, war, natural disasters, and climate change and sustainability.

Politics and Policies

The most disruptive aspect of the early-twenty-first-century global business environment is the rapid development of large emerging markets such as China, India, and Brazil. Throughout the last two decades of the twentieth and the first decade of the twenty-first centuries, these nations appeared to be merging into the liberal world economic order smoothly, easing their political differences with the established industrial world. The emergence of China, in particular, as a reliable site for low-cost manufacturing was the single most important driver of the development of GVCs. With its seemingly infinite supply of low-paid, low-skill but literate, trainable, and tractable workers, China became "the world's workshop" during the 1990s. Economies of scale, low labor costs, location efficiencies, and government support made the manufacture of everything from T-shirts to computers for worldwide markets dependent on outsourcing specialists in China.

The massive flows of foreign exchange into China to pay for all these bargain goods drove the transformation of China's economy, society, and government. Chinese workers were poorly paid compared to workers in other countries, but they were paid sufficiently as factory workers (as opposed to farmers) to become consumers, collectively propelling China into the world's largest market for almost everything from T-shirts to computers. At the same time, massive increases in demand, education, and skills drove China into ever more valuable stages of value-adding production processes and raised wages rapidly at every organizational level. On the societal front, young Chinese workers became the world's go-to consumers of clothing, computer games, smartphones, and about everything else that could be purchased. People raised in rural poverty had seemingly overnight attained large disposable incomes, internet access to visions of a wealth-driven lifestyle, and the freedom to buy their way into it. These societal and economic changes spawned new firms like Alibaba and Tencent, based in the information age and run by young entrepreneurs who quickly became wealthy. Yet for all the help this produced for the rise of global capitalism, globalized demand, and global supply chains, clouds formed on the political and economic horizon.

The government and the Chinese Communist Party never fully relinquished political control of the nation. As the country became richer, its leadership began to reassert what they saw as China's natural and historical role as the preeminent economic and political power in East and Southeast Asia, a role that has expanded quickly under the Xi Jinping regime to challenge Western powers, including the United States, throughout the region, particularly through military base expansion in the South China Sea. Threats to forcibly reincorporate Taiwan into mainland China escalated. At the same time, as increased economic freedom at home led to perceived challenges from Chinese business leaders and Western MNFs, internal social and economic control of business and the economy was reestablished. Widely publicized moves against leaders such as Jack Ma of Alibaba cowed the homegrown capitalists. Threats to force foreign multinationals out of the Chinese market humbled those companies and gave the Chinese access to their technologies, brands, foreign markets, and money.

China's regional political and military expansionism challenged the liberal assumption that encouraging Chinese participation in the global economic system would result in increasingly liberal politics. The Trump administration responded by establishing punitive tariffs on US imports from China and limitations on the export of technology to Chinese companies, policies that the Biden administration has largely maintained and even enhanced. While the Americans saw these policies as natural responses intended to slow the rise of a potentially important rival, the Chinese leadership interpreted them as an effort to prevent China from assuming its rightful natural position as the dominant force in East Asia and the Western Pacific Ocean region. Today, the Xi regime continues its political threats, but has increased its efforts to assert its dominance through economic means to include restricting inward investment, threatening suppliers, limiting Western business services, using its large foreign exchange surpluses to fund investments in Central Asia, Africa, and increasingly in South America, and developing homegrown IT rather than relying on US-sourced hardware and software. The threat of a second Cold War between the Western democracies and a now China-centric coalition in Asia has become real.

Additionally, new assertiveness on the part of India, Brazil, Saudi Arabia, and the UAE, and various other countries increases the existential threat to the post–World War II liberal economic world order. Indeed, in the summer of 2023 the "BRICS" – Brazil, Russia, India, China, and South Africa – have not only begun to meet and act in concert, but they have invited half-a-dozen other mid-sized emerging economies to join them. Near and actual defaults by Greece,

Argentina, Venezuela, and other debtor countries show that the system is as afraid of "the nuclear option" as are the countries in question. Constantly lower tariffs, deference to private capital, forced acceptance of rules imposed by stronger countries despite the pain they create for local constituents, a sense that in the end, everyone would be better off – all of these expectations are called into question. And if we are not all going to do better by adhering to common rules, what then is to be done? We emphasize China's increasing assertiveness, but this pattern is likewise apparent in India, throughout South America, and in Africa – clearly change is in progress, and the outcomes are highly uncertain.

The challenges produced by these developments have a significant impact on MNEs and pose a new version of an age-old management challenge: *how to balance political demands that production be moved and distributed to local suppliers in the MNF's many markets with the evolving insight that economic advantage derives from centralizing and locating assets based on comparative advantage of nations and regions?* The dominant logic in the West has largely viewed fragmented value chains based on specialization across nations and regions as drivers of both excellence and low costs. However, pressures to reverse the flows of production to offshore sites based on political expediency had been building for years and are now accelerating. Historically, MNEs were able to resist political pressures by pointing to more available, less expensive, goods and services for all, even if some workers lost jobs to less expensive labor in the BEMs of Asia. But that resistance breaks down as governments become increasingly aggressive and, in some cases, hostile to global companies. As borders close, either to imports or to exports, alternative sources of supply may turn out to be inadequate or nonexistent. For example, high tariffs on steel imports to the United States had little impact on an American industry that was not prepared to expand (but was happy to take profits when the price of foreign steel jumped). In the end, American products made with more expensive foreign and domestic steel became noncompetitive in foreign markets and lost sales to higher prices at home. Where to locate production while balancing political expediency and economic advantage remains a continuing challenge for managerial decision-makers.

War: Politics by Other Means

Violence, revolution, and invasion are a recurring element of the global business environment with potentially dramatic implications for MNFs. Neither Russia nor Ukraine was a major supplier of technology to world markets in 2022 but were both major suppliers of more traditional commodities. As fighting and blockade halted the flow of Ukrainian wheat out of its Black Sea ports, grain and bread prices spiked around the world, and vulnerable people faced hunger and starvation. Blockade and boycotts halted the flow of Russian oil and natural gas to Western Europe, driving up prices in world markets dramatically – for most everything, as shipping became more costly and raised the cost of virtually all goods just as demand began to recover from the COVID-19 shutdown. Even as the Russia–Ukraine war moves toward a new phase of Ukrainian counterattack in the spring and summer of 2023, it appears to have instigated or encouraged unexpected trends that are likely to outlast the shooting stage. For one, the Eastern boundary of Europe, and perhaps NATO itself, seems likely to be drawn at the Russian and Byelorussian border. The countries of Eastern Europe, despite a rising tide of authoritarianism, have little apparent interest in falling into a neo-Soviet sphere. At the same time, China seems eager to trade its production and technology to Russia in exchange for weapons, gas, and oil. Should this alliance continue to build, the ex-Soviet states of Central Asia, already prime targets of the Chinese Belt and Road Initiative, may be unable to remain independent. Africa is experiencing a spate of coups d'état, military interventions by Russia's Wagner Group, and Chinese investments without regard to human rights abuses. Iran, too, seems to have thrown its lot in with Russia to stave off Western pressures on its nuclear program and human rights concerns, potentially drawing the Middle East into the conflict. These new coalitions were developing anyway, but the war, by putting severe pressure on Russia, has created pressures for faster and deeper involvements, and potential integration, on all sides.

While Russian success in Ukraine could encourage China toward unilateral aggression in dealing with Taiwan, Southeast Asia, and the South China Sea area, it is unlikely that Ukrainian success will end these concerns. Negotiated settlement could have a similar effect, with China encouraged by even moderate step-by-step progress in the Russian agenda. Russian needs for political and economic support seem likely to combine with a national suspicion of the West to provide ever-greater incentives to find an alternative economic partner to the European Union and other Western states. Acceptance of a balanced relationship with China – even economic client status balanced by a stronger nuclear force and much larger natural resource endowment – may well combine with Chinese ambitions to consolidate an Asian core able to ignore or fend off pressures from Europe, isolated America, and stagnated India, while competing for ties in Africa and other developing regions. Chinese desire for regional political dominance has already had significant effects on the economics and politics of the Southeast Asia and Pacific region, but increasing threats of military action, driven by significant expansion of China's base structure and Russian military expansionism are forcing countries and companies that rely on exports from China, Taiwan, and other East and Southeast Asian countries to reevaluate their supply chains. Thus, the USA and Western Europe propose large government subsidies for semiconductor chip plants and battery manufacturing facilities while ratcheting up their controls on the export of commercial and military technologies, due to explicit concerns for military action by China in the region.

Managing political risk is not a new concern for MNEs. The risk of expropriation has been, and continues to be, endemic for modern multinational operations. However, the persistence and threat of all-out war as well as limited regional skirmishes pose an immediate challenge for today's companies, especially to those familiar with the realities of previous wars. *How can MNFs manage the tension between maintaining neutrality in the various conflicts and also serve the demands and exploit the opportunities posed by the several combatants, stakeholders, and victims?* The defense industry has an interest in these questions, but so do a wide variety of ancillary technology and service industries. *Is neutrality desirable or even possible and what happens to assets, subsidies, and expatriate and local employees when countries mobilize and conduct wars?* Historical and popular approaches of "regulatory capture" and "stakeholder management" seem unlikely to be entirely effective in these circumstances. Issues of national identity and loyalty, ethics and morality are not insignificant and cannot be ignored.

Natural Disasters and Their Secondary Consequences

A ubiquitous feature of life is the relative randomness of natural disasters, including, but not limited to, earthquakes, tsunamis, fires, monsoons, tornadoes, hurricanes, and pandemics. Disasters like these have always been with us and will undoubtedly continue to do so. Related to these are the man-made disasters that may be a consequence of these natural phenomenon. Recent decades have seen several examples of this secondary result in major geographically specific disruptions, due to local primary disasters. A well-researched and reported recent example is the earthquake and tsunami that struck central Japan in 2011. Hitting a heavily industrialized region, the double disaster disrupted supply chains for months, especially for Japanese manufacturing, in some cases also impacting worldwide production. These natural phenomena caused a secondary disaster, the nuclear meltdown at Fukushima, which both cut off power to the region and spread radioactive waste over the area, extending the local production shutdown indefinitely. Poorly considered human decisions regarding the location of the plant exacerbated what were fundamentally natural disasters.

Central Japan is subject to frequent severe earthquakes and, somewhat less often, associated tsunami. Of course, Japan has strict building codes and a large, if inadequate, seawall intended to withstand tsunami runs along much of the coast, including to the seaward of the nuclear plants. Given the high probability of such a disaster one must wonder about the willingness of government and industry to place sole source plants in the region. Of course, all of Japan is equally active seismically, so to some extent the risk is unavoidable, but even for domestic markets, multiple plants spread along the thousand-mile chain of islands might have been a wise hedge, spreading risk. And this is far from the only case where predictable natural disasters have overcome industries engaged in "whistling past the graveyard" decision-making. The same year as the Japanese disaster, floods in Thailand swamped plants along the Chao Praya River that were the primary suppliers to the world of low-tech, but critical, components like capacitors and resistors for the assembly of computers and cellphones in China, shuttering production for weeks.

While local disasters can cause unexpected difficulties in the case of very specific production of a very specific item, the COVID-19 pandemic is an example of the impact of a *worldwide* natural disaster (the natural spread of the SARS2 virus was the real disaster, even if the virus itself turns out to be the product of a lab in China). As with most such disasters, the problems are as much in the responses to it as in the disaster itself. The deaths of millions and the severe illness of possibly a billion or more people are tragic. Moreover, societal and government responses caused severe disruptions in economies, cultures, and societies. The secretive nature of the Chinese government exacerbated the rapid spread of the disease – and subsequent draconian efforts to limit its spread domestically virtually shut down world trade in several critical areas, and later sudden abandonment of any controls brought a rapidly moving national epidemic that further disrupted trade for much of a year. At the same time, widely disparate efforts at quarantine in most developed countries halted much trade, virtually stopped international travel, destroyed companies, cost jobs, drove the current inflationary cycle, and set a generation of children back years in their schooling. In many of the least developed countries, weak to nonexistent government resulted in minimal organized responses, but surprisingly low levels of infection and death, apparently due to less internal and external travel. MNFs have had to respond much more quickly. The vulnerability of global supply lines to large-scale shutdowns of ports, shipping, and other transport quickly became apparent. Ships piled up at ports in southern California and other hubs in market countries, while closed factories quickly shut down the flow of goods out of China and other offshoring centers. Goods became unavailable, and then as safety measures were put in place for truckers and warehouse workers, the bloated networks were drained, while restarting production proved to be problematic. Only recently has the subsequent inflation in goods prices in the United States and Western Europe begun to moderate.

For MNEs, the central imperative in the face of both natural disasters and their potential secondary disastrous consequences revolves around issues of preparedness and risk reduction. While secondary effects are relatively predictable, the timing and extent of natural disasters are less amenable to prediction. *How can companies hedge against the likelihood of disaster? Is insurance an adequate hedge against the cost of disaster? How can poor, often myopic, decision-making be avoided? How can organizational infrastructure be distributed to ensure continuous operations without sacrificing scale and location advantages?*

Global Warming, Climate Change, and the Environment

Perhaps the most critical feature of the current chaotic environment, one that is related to but underlies many of the other natural and man-made disasters, is the existential crisis of climate change and its implications for global warming. The overwhelming majority of scientists in relevant fields consider increases in temperatures worldwide to be driven by people-made generation of greenhouse gases, particularly carbon dioxide from burning fossil fuels, but also methane from natural gas production and agriculture and other chemicals from various processes. Individual companies and industries, and at least some national governments, are only now adjusting to the idea that a warmer Earth is a real threat to life and to the idea that humans can actually do something about this threat. Unfortunately, science also suggests that even major changes in greenhouse gas production will have only gradual effects, so that a warmer climate appears unavoidable over the next century or more, and only reversible if levels of these gases can be reduced significantly. Changes in power generation, manufacturing, transportation and travel, heating and cooling of buildings, agricultural practices, even in information storage and processing – essentially any activity that requires energy inputs – are going to be necessary, requiring massive investments and behavioral changes. Whether adaptation can happen quickly enough to maintain populations and to provide ever-improving lives is unclear. What is clear is that minor adjustments with the goal of a return to the status quo will not be adequate. Collectively, all may need to adjust to higher sea levels and hotter climates and less water and more fires indefinitely, or we may hopefully see improvement, even reversal, of current trends. In either case, it is a certainty that technology, culture, and human endeavor will be different on the other end of this crisis than they were in the last century.

In the face of these potentially catastrophic threats *what role can MNFs play? How can companies balance the need to be responsible citizens, contributing to greenhouse gas reductions through policies like carbon transfers, reductions in emissions, recycling of goods and inputs to the production process, and managing the organizational infrastructure, while enhancing productivity and competitiveness with companies without such environmental commitments? Should companies organize for environmental responsiveness through dedicated departments responsible for environmental policy and practice or through processes of dispersion of responsibility for these issues throughout the organization? Would hybrid responses be more effective?* UNEP, The Unite Nations Environmental Program, while an active source of guidance and leadership, is limited in how much it can demand and/or enforce. Partnerships with activists, governments, and other interested actors can help but are unlikely to be effective absent a comprehensive government/private sector partnership. *What role should MNFs play as potential advocates for change and improvement when profitability and market share may be at risk?*

5 Adaptive Responses at the Firm Level and the GMBF Model

Has the GMBF concept failed in the face of these challenges? Or did mistaken assumptions and bad implementation simply get caught out by events? The latter interpretation seems more plausible. Building networks of suppliers working on relatively short-term contracts was supposed to create an efficient, responsive, resilient, and agile system of supply and innovation, with global systems integration able to shift production of inputs and outputs quickly in response to changing conditions. Unfortunately, complex transnational network organizations were overlaid on the previous hierarchical system during a relatively long period of economic stability, which let the demands of efficiency drive out slack and therefore limit resilience. As various production sites were closed to the world by natural disasters, such as the Japanese tsunami or Thai floods, or by man-made troubles, such as the poorly considered Japanese nuclear reactor design or poorly designed tariff increases by populist regimes and pressures for geopolitical dominance, systemic weaknesses were exposed. Value supply and distribution networks were challenged by the global COVID-19 pandemic, shut down at the source, backed up at ports, and starved by production shutdown. Geopolitics interferes with both these and also with technological innovation as the USA tries to limit the flow of technology to China and the flows of goods, investment, and internet apps from China, and China cracks down on investment, intellectual property, and foreign companies looking at the Chinese market. And, in the end, lower costs and easier accessibility still matter a lot.

Firm-level responses to these challenges have varied along three dimensions: value production and logistics; innovation and adaptability; and sustainability and environmental responsiveness. We see challenges in all areas, but we consider that the GMBF is a superior organizational model than the alternatives in the current chaotic environment. The multinational is perhaps more able to separate markets from each other, but it does not offer the benefits of global assets. The transnational, while it seeks the benefits of global presence, retains the restrictions of ownership that put firms, and not just their operations in different countries, at risk. The GMBF model (if not always its application) benefits from geographically dispersed and organizationally decentralized value-adding operations and markets, while using technology and branding to gain global, not just multi-local, advantage. By minimizing ownership, except when clearly beneficial, the GMBF avoids putting its assets at risk while using incentives and technology to keep its many components in order.

Value-Production and Logistics Systems

Surprisingly, in a world of many suppliers, certain key components for many industries were ultimately sourced from a single location and, indeed, often from the same company, so that seeming redundancy and adaptability was an illusion. As the Russian cosmonaut in the movie *Armageddon* (1998) put it bluntly: "American components, Russian components, all made in Taiwan!" Perhaps he could have added "all made in Taiwan ... by the Taiwan Semiconductor Manufacturing Company (TSMC)" as a sole source in a single country!

Even as the array of sources feeding GVCs shrank, ownership as a necessity for strategic control seemed increasingly obsolete as digital information technologies narrowed the field by eliminated information asymmetries in deal making, making moral hazard both visible and easily punished, and rendering compliance and operations monitoring inexpensive and ubiquitous.

As a prime example, when COVID-19 shut down many markets for goods and disrupted supply chains, demand dropped suddenly for many commodities. In response, and as national policy shut manufacturing sites to control the disease, producers slowed the production of semiconductor chips, among many other key industrial components, dramatically. When demand for consumer goods surged in 2021, suddenly the firms that made the many products that used these chips as components, most notably automobiles, could not restart manufacturing until the chip foundries could be cranked back up and their own supply chains restarted. Industry discovered that terminating contracts and shutting down foundries could be done much more quickly than revving production back up and starting the supply chains moving again. The systemic resilience that was touted widely right up until COVID-19 struck was discovered to be largely fictional.

Pressures for efficiency and technology have left the world in a situation where a small number of companies makes most of the world supply of many commodity-like inputs in a limited number of massively large, highly sophisticated, and very capital-intensive fabrication facilities in only a few locations – such as computer chips in China, Taiwan, and South Korea. No matter what companies were contracted by Ford, BMW, or Geely (or Apple, Samsung, and Sony) to supply various chips, actual manufacture of these key components lay in the hands of these few "fabricators." And they had stopped production when contracts dried up and then faced long delays in increasing supply when demand suddenly surged across virtually all goods-producing and chip-using industries. So, Americans, Europeans, Japanese, Indians, and other customers who suddenly wanted that new car once they felt they could start leaving home again simply could not get one. And the price of used cars jumped dramatically as this latent demand shifted, and, well, the story is well known. What does this mean for the future of MNFs?

The cost of production technology had made excess capacity for chip production irrational – at least while the system worked smoothly – so redundancy in both chip suppliers and production locations had been eliminated from the system. Excess capacity, stockpiles, inventory, truly redundant suppliers, and production facilities – all were driven out by the relentless demand for better technology at a lower cost. At the same time, the need for chips to operate systems within many products – cars, entertainment, even blenders, and services – especially server farms for cloud computing and cryptocurrencies – kept demand expanding steadily. When the system was jammed by unexpected events, it simply did not have the slack to adapt to sudden changes. With no inventory capacity due to companies' avoidance of working capital charges, slowdowns required decommissioning production, so that sudden increases had no stock to draw from – and restarting production was slow and problematic. So too was restarting the shipping system, with shortages and chokepoints from one end to the other preventing a smooth recovery and unfulfilled demand leading to price inflation as consumers bid against each other for – well, pretty much everything. Logistical systems intended to be maximally efficient through the application of just-in-time principles to global supply chains had been working just fine in the long period of expansion but were unable to deal with sudden drops and surges in demand resulting from trade wars and COVID-19 (Buttonwood, 2022). Volatility was unexpected and unprepared for.

We see these principles applied in a variety of cases around the world. In manufacturing, global supply chains based on outsourced production, often in less developed or emerging market countries, have become standard in industries from sport shoes to smartphones. Indeed, the emphasis on offshoring much manufacturing value creation to China has impacted manufacturing in the United States (both in fact and in imagination) to such an extent that it is the driver of the Trump administration's tariff wars with that country and a precipitating factor in the politically driven supply chain crisis. The use of strategic assembly and animation in services is less obvious but is becoming ever more useful in information-based professional services mid-sized companies worldwide. The strategic systems of multinational companies must find the right balance between efficiency and resilience in the face of an ever-more volatile, uncertain, complex, and ambiguous global business environment and constantly rising competitive pressures.

As the increasingly frictionless world of trade and investment that engendered the Global Factory (Buckley and Ghauri, 2004) disappears, MNFs are finding the need for insurance against sudden – or not so sudden – delays and disruptions. They need to be prepared for increasing frictions in international transactions at the political, social, and economic levels while experiencing increasingly transparent information. It seems likely that operations will be forced to decentralize into multiple locations, both to satisfy nationalist demand for local production and to relieve the potential for supply disruption that is inherent to single point sourcing. Again, Buckley et al. (2022) predict increasing barriers to trade in both final and intermediate goods, slowing offshoring to low wage economies, while environmental concerns are likely to slow globalization of goods production, but the "work from home" ethos of the COVID-19 era may encourage further dispersal and offshoring of intellectual services. They conclude that the rents to intangible assets are likely to rise, while tangible assets will begin to accumulate near their markets rather than in offshore production centers.

In one encouraging sign, MNFs are diversifying their production sites. Multinational manufacturers are said to be taking a "China plus one" approach to production (Swanson, 2023), meaning that they are moving production, especially for the US market, to Mexico, Vietnam, and other lower-cost countries. This second source requirement has been a feature of defense contacting for many years. Chinese companies, such as Shien, TikTok, and Jinko Solar, are also following similar strategies (Swanson, 2023). Jinko Solar, the largest producer of solar panels in the world today, has production in a dozen countries

(Swanson, 2023), and has set up supply and production chains for the US market that are entirely outside China, even as American politicians threaten their access. Similarly, TikTok is stressing that it is building a "firewall" between its US company and Chinese parent ByteDance, and Shien, Haier, and other manufacturers are emphasizing their offshoring investments in the United States and other countries outside their Chinese homeland. Even so, *The Economist* (2023f) reports that while direct trade from China to the United States has dropped in the first half of 2023, China's exports to and investments in America's suppliers in Mexico, Vietnam, Taiwan, and India are rising fast. As "decoupling" policies have forced production for the United States and Western Europe out of China, these "friend shoring" sites have become more dependent on China for their parts and intermediate goods. *The Economist* concludes that trade links remain despite policy efforts to end them but have become more complex and expensive.

Natural disasters also are less predictable – the political differences between the United States and China have been decades in the making, and, while hardly offering a monotonic path toward confrontation, have also become increasingly apparent. Earthquakes and volcanic eruptions, on the other hand, still offer little or no warning, while the paths of hurricanes and cyclones are predictable only over a few days or weeks. However, these events tend to occur much more often in some places than others – the Pacific Ring of Fire, the Bay of Bengal, the Gulf of Mexico, along the world's major rivers. They also tend to occur in cycles or with a degree of statistical predictability. A major earthquake and tsunami in central Japan is no surprise, though the size of the 2011 events was larger than usual. Hurricanes in Florida and the Bay of Bengal are nearly annual occurrences, and wildfires in Australia and California are to be expected. MNFs need to cut through the man-made fog of contracts and subcontracts, assurances that "it can't happen ... again," and government boosterism to know where their supply chains originate from and run through and to ensure that they are not vulnerable to a single event, especially an event that is to be expected, even if the exact timing is not.

Of course, region-wide or global disasters such as COVID-19 are more difficult to dodge by diversification of production sites, especially when they strike at the logistical system as much as the production system. While COVID-19 affected the world, it was not equally severe everywhere and peak impact timing varied from place to place. The response of "just shut everything down everywhere" probably hurt societies, cultures, and industries and companies, more than the actual disease. Given that the conditions that fanned the pandemic are increasingly understood – but very difficult to avoid in the future – governments and companies need to put in place plans to deal with similar events in the

future. If we can't just shift production to another emerging economy to avoid
a disruptive event, how can we be prepared? Flexibility and adaptability are
clearly required, as is contingency planning that does not assume a benign
global environment and easily contained crises. A deeper understanding of
who is truly essential is critical, as are clearly understood alternatives to the
system in place, as complex as they may be. Increases in data collection,
computing power, and software performance might well offer the possibility
of contingency planning on the required scale. Perhaps artificial intelligence
(AI) can find a purpose in the strategy of logistics as well as the operation. The
strategic value of Big Data may become apparent.

All of the drivers of locational risk point to one key solution for increased
resilience – more, and more diversified, production sites. Assembly of MNF
value chains needs not only to propound the importance of resilience, it
needs to ensure that the organization actually offers it. Gradual movement
away from China-only manufacturing has begun, but clearly needs to accelerate. Re-shoring or near-shoring, returning production back home or near
home (usually within a regional trade agreement), tends to reduce political
risks to the system but may still leave production at risk from natural
disasters. MNFs likely will have little choice but to move more final assembly to their market regions, but should ensure coordination across regions so
that disruptions in one location can be temporarily offset by slack built into
another. They also need to encourage their suppliers to diversify and de-risk
their own supply chains. Simply lengthening their supply chain roots while
having them continue to draw from the same Chinese well will not help
MNFs in the case of a political standoff. Which emphasizes the obvious –
a requisite amount of slack capacity simply must be estimated and accepted.
Systems will break down due to both internal and external events, and
resilience and flexibility require slack resources. As we have seen with
chips, adapting the system by closing and restarting production is not
a viable solution in many industries, inventories must be considered in the
light of options and contingent values, not simply seen as expensive liabil-
ities. Warehousing of inputs, intermediate goods, and final products at
different locations along global and regional supply lines is needed.

As MNFs seek multiple sites, they also must consider the value of multiple
partners. Relying on single suppliers, even if they have multiple production
sites, ignores the potential for political influence, disasters impacting headquarters functions, and for unbalanced priorities. Strategic assembly concepts are
designed to address these needs for multiple suppliers in multiple locations;
strategic animation principles mean that market forces can be used to keep all
participants in a global value chain focused on the same outcomes without

returning to extensive ownership positions in all parts of the global value chain. MNFs may indeed find that they may want to internalize one operation or another for specific reasons, but trying to manage widespread and redundant operations internally is neither feasible nor desirable. As we have seen, global supply chains can be disrupted by failure in the smallest, most obscure, most apparently peripheral link, and even traditional MNFs never owned and controlled everything. Rather, the need for continued investment in communication and coordination has become apparent. Animation of networks of suppliers and distributors requires clarity of communication and coordination driven by both trust and incentives. What is not under any serious discussion is vertical integration by industrial firms into the world of semiconductor manufacturing. Perhaps a few chip design and marketing firms could acquire fabrication facilities, but Toyota or Boeing or Apple are not because no user has the levels of demand to run a captive fab at an economic scale. Moreover, the processes and capabilities required are recognized to be completely foreign. Better contracts or improved supply lines are needed, global ownership and bureaucracies are not.

At the same time, MNFs that have coordinated production along their highly efficient JIT systems may want to consider the value of trading companies. Once among the most valuable firms worldwide, Japanese *sogo shosha* (a type of trading company) and companies like them have become less important when flagship MNFs ran their worldwide operations as Buckley's global factories (Buckley and Ghauri, 2004; Buckley et al., 2022). However, as GVCs slow, inventories are gathered at various locations, more value providers are incorporated, and other inefficiencies are incorporated to build resilience, specialists in network coordination and goods transfer seem likely to become needed partners. Does the Information Age lead to the Age of Logistics and can they successfully coexist?

Innovation

Besides redefining the balance of efficiency and resiliency, this newly chaotic era seems likely to force reconsideration of the role and sources of innovation, both product and process, and in both goods production and service provision. MNFs had for some time been extending their R&D facilities away from their home countries – as a purely HQ function – into regional neighbors and further into worldwide locations. General Electric, for instance, had established primary innovation sites in Europe, but also as far afield as China, well known as the source of GE's portable ultrasound units (Immelt et al., 2009). Microsoft had labs in China, too, and IBM looked to India for innovative solutions, while

Geely of China invested in Volvo of Sweden as much to acquire cutting-edge automotive technology as to access Volvo's markets. Mazda located its design and development for the successful MX-5 (Miata) model to southern California, an area known for its passion for open topped roadsters. MNFs had long recognized that demand varied from market to market, and had established laboratories for product development in many regions and countries. By the early 2000s, though, with the rise of the BEMs as both markets and production sites, more firms recognized that unique cultural and technological settings could provide technology with potentially global implications, and had begun to take note of innovation from outside the home country and even from established lead subsidiaries (Bartlett and Ghoshal, 1989). Even more, leading MNFs established primary research facilities with the intention of creating world-class innovation in disparate locations and tying them together through ICT-reliant oversight. Core facilities were typically owned by the MNF; others were set up as joint ventures with local partners.

At the same time, emerging MNFs from less advanced nations began to pursue actively technological innovation in and from the industrialized economies of the West. As mentioned, Geely bought Volvo, but also Tata Motors of India bought Jaguar-LandRover in Britain and pursued a variety of joint ventures with European, Japanese, and Korean firms to bring up-to-date automotive technology to India. On the process side, Uniqlo of Japan invested considerable capital, both financial and human, in training their Chinese suppliers in Japanese production methods (Yen, 2016). Chinese firms have been particularly focused on acquiring knowledge from elsewhere. Manufacturing in China often involves local partners, and under Chinese regulatory pressure, foreign MNFs must share their technology with these partners, and in the case of wholly owned subsidiaries, with the government. In various industries, innovation that originated in the USA or Western Europe has been incorporated and brought to market in and then from China. Thus, much of the innovative technology in solar power was developed in the United States, but Chinese subsidies of production and local markets (contrasted with US politics-driven resistance to commercial solar power) have allowed Chinese firms to dominate the market while many of the originating American firms have disappeared. Likewise, Chinese firms dominate the market for wind power equipment, building on Western technology, both purchased and acquired through theft and espionage. In response, the US government has begun to limit the export of key technology, such as advanced chip design, to China or Chinese companies, and has also blocked the acquisition of American technology firms by Chinese MNFs. The Chinese government has retaliated by restricting the export of their own technology, such as that for casting silicon wafers for solar power applications, and also minerals and components needed for production of information technology devices (The Economist, 2023e). Even more recently, China's anticompetition authority has blocked the acquisition of Tower Semiconductors of Israel Intel by refusing to rule on its acceptability in China, a major market for Intel, but where Tower has only a small presence (Clark and Bradsher, 2023). Governments are trying to limit dependencies on foreign countries for innovation and technology, while also trying to encourage and subsidize local innovation.

MNFs are responding to such pressures by building both production and innovation in key markets. Taiwan Semiconductor Manufacturing Company (TSMC) has committed to building chip foundries in the United States and Western Europe, while keeping its most advanced production and its R&D in Taiwan. TikTok and other Chinese firms are working to convince Western regulators that they can operationally separate their home units from local host units and prevent any flow of customer information across borders, while continuing to share software innovations across these units. Tesla has significant facilities in the United States and China, and is rapidly expanding in Europe. Already, pundits are looking at differences in AI development in the United States and China and asking if they can possibly be compatible (Andersen, 2023). Will innovative technologies in battery design, autonomous driving, or electrical drives be shared across these boundaries, or will companies need to restrict innovative efforts to single countries or regions? Will China allow Tesla to share innovations developed in its market, perhaps with local partners, to be incorporated into US designs and production? Will the USA allow tech transfer within the firm but across unfriendly borders? As China threatens retaliation against firms that are caught in sanctions efforts by the United States and other governments, Tesla and other Western firms may question their commitment to innovation in China if their intellectual property – or even their entire operation – can be acquired or shut down. Importing technology to China that might be seized will certainly raise concerns. Chinese (and Indian, as well) firms in the rest of the world may find that acquisition of technology licenses or even local firms to access cutting-edge technology that they desire to share or take home – a problem for them and for innovators hoping to cash out. The United States is happy to get Chinese investment and access to Chinese markets, but has realized that offering easy access to technology and other innovations to China, India, and other BEMs is subsidizing the development of strong competitors. Government subsidy underlies much commercial innovation – how do firms respond to demands to restrict such innovation to local or regional friendly markets? Can companies restrict some, but not all, organizational learning between and within companies voluntarily or will external control become more common?

How can MNFs respond to new restrictions on the flow of information? In the case of political and military rivalries, companies may need to separate their operational entities completely – perhaps maintaining a holding company to monitor financial status, but with very limited flows of information and product across hot borders. Of course, managing a set of independent national subsidiaries hardly plays to the strengths of modern networked MNFs. The inability to share information and innovation limits returns to what can be very large investments and so will likely slow or stop much innovation. Even without strong government limitations, pressures to reveal innovative technology, product, or process to partners/ rivals without legal protection can cause global networks of innovation to collapse. ICT, medical innovations, transportation, power generation, and many other tech-heavy areas are critical to both military and commercial innovation, and practically are "dual-use" to some degree. Thus, efforts to assemble networks for innovation will require both technological considerations and sophisticated understanding of the requirements and limitations of major sites for both the development and the marketing of innovation and innovative products. Animation seems an attractive model for motivating the developers of intellectual property, but regulatory requirements, government intervention, incompatible expectations, and other areas of profound disagreement about innovation may well require nuanced approaches that adapt to diverse intellectual environments. As Andersen (2023) says about AI, this innovative technology could well offer significant advantage to the country or national system that moves fastest – and systems are likely to be different in different locations.

The most likely immediate consequences of disruptions to global markets and supply lines are that the largest MNFs will begin to focus on national or regional R&D, reducing sharing to the most fundamental and innovative concepts while developing these independently in different locations. Innovation will be tied ever more closely to markets, very possibly slowing technology development, including that needed for responses to pandemics and other health crises. In the longer term, and in the event of higher levels of confrontation, firms may be forced to leave unfriendly markets, sell off to local rivals, or completely separate their operations, to include listing local subsidiaries only on local exchanges. As with production and trade, regional groupings of friendly (or at least cooperating) countries like Schengen partners in Western Europe may circumscribe the geographical scope of innovation. Smaller markets will likely slow innovation. Since information is relatively easy and cheap to move, espionage is likely to flourish, further limiting the value of new ideas. MNFs are likely to resist state limitations on knowledge development and transfer, but in the end cannot ignore them, and even highly diversified networks will struggle if too many links are cut or closed where they cross borders. As some analysts have observed (Clark and Bradsher, 2023), MNFs such as Intel may soon be forced to decide whether to operate in China or in the rest of the world and the role of China could be substituted by most large markets.

Sustainability and Environmental Responsiveness

Demands for sustainability in the face of natural pressures (disease, but also climate change, sea rise, air and water pollution, and population trends) and distributive justice in the face of income inequality, health care inequities, and employment restructuring and uncertainty will increase the complexity of cross-border operations and require increasing innovation and resilience on the part of companies. The new global strategic organizations will be active and empowered citizens of the new economic order. Everyone has an interest in how they exercise their franchise.

Additionally, regionalization and re- or near-shoring should reduce the length and energy intensiveness of supply chains. Costs will rise as production returns to industrial nations, but increasing use of computers and information technology, including AI, flexible production, increased automation of factories and transport, and the like are likely to make labor costs largely irrelevant. This process may well be driven by political necessity, but can also reduce the energy requirements for production of goods by reducing the length of supply lines and by easing the process of removing fossil fuels from industrial transport (sea and air transport being the most difficult to convert to batteries or other forms of sustainable power).

However, while energy costs and carbon intensiveness may be reduced by shortened supply lines, other environmental costs may become increasingly relevant. Rare earth minerals for electronics and lithium, needed for rechargeable batteries, are widely distributed, but production today is concentrated in China and a few developing countries because it is environmentally destructive and expensive to mitigate. Chip production requires large amounts of water, which is a challenge in drier parts of the United States. In addition, the industrial market countries have extensive regulatory protection for communities and individuals, requiring lengthy and uncertain permitting procedures, which lowers flexibility and raises costs. MNFs may be unwilling or unable to suffer such costs while remaining competitive, but it is not clear whether countries that want local production of these critical inputs to technological products will offer relief or price protection.

Then, of course, as we indicated earlier, there is the persistence and ubiquity of climate change – and sea level rise, glacial melting, changes in weather patterns, and the rest of the symptoms of a warmer world. Most of the world's major cities are on coastlines and will see flooding that will range from inconvenient to catastrophic. Others, such as Phoenix, Arizona in the United States, are already beginning to limit growth because they are in danger of running out of water. While global threats cannot be avoided, they can be addressed at the level of the firm. First, companies must reconsider their choices of location given the new situation. The likelihood and scope of sea level rise, for instance, are not new, but estimates have evolved over time to suggest that this phenomenon will be faster and greater than previously hypothesized, and perhaps most disconcerting, probably cannot be stopped or significantly slowed or reduced for many decades, even if atmospheric greenhouse gas concentration growth can be halted or reversed. Heat gain will take considerable time to peak and reverse, even in the face of extreme responses – which we see little reason to anticipate. Firms will need to either harden sites or move away from coastal areas. Likewise, locations that are most vulnerable to severe weather or seasonal flooding may become untenable, or at least uninsurable. It is already difficult to insure homes in parts of Florida. Such moves may also involve adjustment to new political realities, such that re-shoring of chip manufacturing, for instance, may include consideration of water supplies – considerable water is used in manufacturing integrated circuits – as well as labor, power, and tax abatements. Supply chains need to become more flexible as key locations change, and existing port and land transport facilities become problematic.

Industry can begin to work to mitigate warming through changes in norms and company policies. For instance, it appears that the majority of cars and trucks will be powered by electricity within a few decades, despite a lack of regulatory requirement. As the costs of solar power and other sustainable energy sources drop, it is also likely that industrial, commercial, and private buildings will transition to electrical power and to either on-site generation and storage or to a sustainably sourced grid. Of course, new compromises will be required – production of solar panels and batteries is polluting, if in new ways. Wind power generation is harmful to birds and views, and vulnerable to its own natural disasters. Nuclear plants may become vital sources of a stable base supply, as may major dams. Both sources have strong opponents, often among the community that pushes hardest to end fossil fuel use. While the likely trend is toward sustainable power, it is clearly a solution that will take place at different rates in different places, and will probably see politically driven setbacks and enhancements. Choices of technology and location and diversification of both are likely to be essential for industry for many years to come – all outcomes that should be eased by the flexibility and responsiveness inherent to the GMBF concept.

MNFs must continue to support alternative sources of power for production and for transportation, but it seems unlikely that most consumers, especially in the United States, will be willing to pay significantly higher prices for green initiatives, at least today. However, it also seems likely that climate change will become such an undeniable crisis in the relatively near future, that firms will likely be better off to begin to adjust now rather than waiting for sudden stringent regulation – building in flexibility in sourcing, transportation, and direction of innovation is likely to demonstrate time-scale economies (Dierickx and Cool, 1989), and those who hold out until forced to change may not survive. The GMBF should be able to use the principles of animation to motivate affiliated firms to engage in environmentally sound practices – we see no need for ownership and enforcement to seek such goals. Indeed, by offering incentives for innovation and for sharing knowledge among their suppliers and distributors, MNFs may be able to use the loosely tied networks of the GMBF model to increase innovation and application of green technologies beyond what the tight control and direction of a traditional multinational firm can engender.

6 What May Tomorrow Bring?

So, can these solutions – and others – be handled by global MNFs and networks going forward, and if so, how? We argue that the answer is yes – and specifically, that the GMBF model offers the most viable solution in the face of multiple forces that have turned the stable global business environment into a volatile and uncertain, if not chaotic, setting. Strategic assembly is intended to build strategic organizations, not just firms, that deliver value to customers – sometimes classic goods and services, but increasingly to provide the value of these classic products to those who need them. By moving away from the ownership-centric bureaucracies and capital investments of the multinational and transnational organization models, the GMBF is intended to be adaptable and responsive to changing circumstances – new locations chosen to handle new political or environmental realities, for instance, or a lack of legal ownership to avoid regulatory red tape, delay, and, at times, liability. It is also intended to enhance innovation, both by encouraging innovation within and between its units with tangible rewards, and in the overall organization by allowing new units to be brought into the network without the cost, delay, and inertia of ownership. If Intel had bid for a global technological and manufacturing partnership with Tower, for instance, it seems unlikely that China (or any other regulator) would have been able to block the transaction as it did the recently failed acquisition.

While the GMBF offers an organizational solution to uncertain, changing, even chaotic environments, we have seen that the central MNFs must work to maintain these advantages in the face of the many unpredictable forces for changes in both direction and pace. Internalizing contractors can be an easy solution to supply or distribution issues in the short term, but eliminates the option value of contracts. Market-like reward structures may seem inordinately expensive in a good year, but they are also likely to be both less costly and more incentivizing in the inevitable not-so-good years to follow. Competitors moving to more strictly efficient supply chains with single sourcing, cost pressures on suppliers, lowest cost locations, and cheap logistics will be a challenge when investors and boards bring pressures to forego innovation, flexibility, and responsiveness, which they inevitably will do. Long-term solutions to long-term or inevitable, but not immediate, problems are difficult to sustain in today's global stock markets dominated economy. Thus, the China-linked third-country supply chains are not surprising – some inputs come only from China today, others are simply much less expensive when sourced from China. While internal mandates could address these issues immediately (at least hypothetically – top management has always struggled to make subsidiaries incur higher costs while rewarding profits), there is no reason to think that incentives and rewards cannot be used to move ultimate suppliers to other countries, especially as more countries subsidize production of inputs as disparate as lithium ore and advanced semiconductor chips.

What do we see in the near future? Political conflict is likely to persist, even if current active wars are brought to an end, and with it economic disruption will escalate. A new bipolar, or perhaps multipolar, political economy seems likely, and MNFs are likely to find that they will have to separate, even wall off, operations in one camp from those in the other(s). Multinational networks seem likely to persist, but will be run in parallel rather than as a single global operation. MNFs will face pressures to separate their operational entities in different political spheres in a convincing manner if the disruptive environment of today continues to worsen. Even more, innovation in technologies that have national strategic implications – chips, AI, energy – seems likely to become subject to restriction. Most electronic hardware and software have military and political implications, and the continued free flow of such knowledge seems unlikely at best. Can firms operate in multiple competing countries? Are internal firewalls adequate? If they are, do they eliminate the benefit of a global position? MNFs are going to have to answer such questions, and are going to have to stay radically responsive to the developing answers. MNFs must begin to develop regional supply networks and to define how they can leverage their IP across not just borders, but across boundaries between incompatible, even competing, political and economic systems.

As a consequence, we expect to see more heterogeneity among firms. One set of global players will likely pursue generalist strategies integrating strategic assembly and animation to produce, market, and sell full product lines, whether in services like Nexia International or intermediate or finished manufacturing goods. In consumer goods, for example, Unilever and Proctor and Gamble will likely compete head-to-head in the full of range business, markets, and products as full line global players. Similarly, L'Oréal, the French-based personal care company, will continue to go to market as a generalist. Other companies will pursue more specialist strategies. We expect to see consolidation within and between companies specializing in assembly and animation. Operators such as Whitbread PLC in the United Kingdom will go to market primarily based on the capability to effectively deliver on the value-adding opportunities of existing assets and businesses in areas like hotels and restaurants. For companies like Whitbread successful animation will become its source of potential competitive advantage. Another group, led by venture capital and private placement special purpose acquisition companies (SPACs), will create value by assembling organizational components in an efficient and effective manner, though mergers, full or partial acquisition, joint ventures, and the like. Over time assemblers will surely need to animate and animators will have to manage assembly and de-assembly, but in the shorter-term specialization may offer effective positioning. In the longer term, acquisition of specialist companies by generalists may become the norm as pressures for growth inhibit specialist profitability.

We anticipate a global business environment that encourages regional and local final goods production and distribution and services controlled by regionally established providers. These firms will be the multinational signature firms for their supply networks, which will be dispersed throughout the region and able to tap other regions when politically and economically feasible. Firms at all levels will look to partnerships with local, national, and regional governing bodies to subsidize production when scale alone is inadequate, provide economic and legal barriers to "cheaters" that source across boundaries, and support innovation so long as it takes place locally. The benefits: less likely political disruption, more direct connections between manufacturing and markets, lower transportation costs (both financial and carbon-footprint), and identification among producers, government, and consumers within the regions. The costs: higher prices in industrialized countries with more expensive labor, more environment protection, more regulatory processes, less variety in most locations as scale economies pressure firms to make more of fewer products, less innovation in many regions where technologies are less advanced and citizens less educated. The tradeoff, the cost-benefit results, will likely be dependent on specific levels of tension and productive capacity. We can only be certain that the assessments will change over time, with no solution permanent. Possibly a very few will even extend beyond the next budgetary cycle.

Concentration of production, while easing the effects of political tensions and likely helping with reducing and adapting to long-term natural disasters, could expose firms to location-based disasters. However, a broader vision of what makes for a good production site, a commitment to dispersion and diversification, application of sustainable production technologies, and the use of technology to enhance communication between and coordination of multiple locations for every stage of value production clearly can avoid most such concerns – presuming that top management has the will to stay the course. Slack is expensive, until it is needed.

Of course, will power and strategic vision have always been in relatively short supply, and financial pressures to maximize short-term gains seem unlikely to abate. We could well exit the current chaotic environment with a newly innovative and flexible model focused on solving long-term problems and avoiding political interference, and, then after a few years of relative calm, find that MNFs have reverted to efficiency in the place of flexibility, avoidance of environmental concerns, and increased risks for yet another uncertain future. We hope not.

7 Will the Multinational Survive? And What Will It Look Like?

A most important lesson to be drawn from our research is that the multidivisional, multinational, firm, one of the most significant of the second industrial revolution innovations, commensurate with the invention and development of electricity, trains, telegraph, and telephones, has been remarkably resilient and adaptive to environmental changes. Driven by the constant drumbeat of political and economic challenges, technological innovations, and competitive threats, the M-Form has evolved from the simple to the more complex, each approach better able to deal with evolving contexts. This process is of particular relevance for international business and MNE behavior. First, the multinational form sought to solve the challenges of managing across borders in scale and scope as companies found international reach brought opportunities for enhanced profitability. Next, the Trans-National organization evolved to solve the challenging requirements of cross-border cooperation as international activities required increasing coordination across units as companies sought to leverage managerial capabilities. Most recently, the Multi-Business model has developed to take advantage of information technology, political complexity and financial market demands for efficiency, effectiveness, and agility, while maintaining profitability and cooperative behavior across units.

The GMBF and its many successes notwithstanding, our current state of multinational strategic management is unlikely to remain stable indefinitely. Change has always been, and will likely continue to be, a key feature of international business. So, will the multinational firm survive? Certainly, the MNF will not wither away any more than the State will cease to be relevant. However, the past does not guarantee success in business any more than it does in finance and investing. A more compelling question that our research has highlighted is, *how* will the multinational survive and what will it look like? Continued adaptability and innovation will be required, and managerial action and thought will be especially important. This insight cannot be overemphasized, nor should it be discounted. Consequently, we propose that the diversified, decentralized multinational firm, built on the GMBF model of strategic assembly and animation, has great advantages. Economies of scope and scale and investment in innovation at the firm level argue for specialization, while advances in ICT permit contractual arrangements to be as functional, and much less costly, as any hierarchical controls. The answer lies not in a new organizational form for the MNF, but in a world of true networks, assembled for efficiency and innovation and animated to deliver on these promises.

References

Andersen, R. 2023. Inside the revolution at open AI. *The Atlantic*, September: 52–76.

Bair, J. 2008. Analyzing economic organization: Embedded networks and global chains compared. *Economy and Society*, 37: 339–364.

Barnard, C. 1938. *The Functions of the Executive*. Cambridge, MA: Harvard University Press.

Bartlett, C. A., and Ghoshal, S. 1989. *Managing across borders: The transnational solution*. Boston, MA: Harvard Business School Press.

Blinder, A. S. 2006. Offshoring: The next industrial revolution? *Foreign Affairs*, 85/2: 113–128.

Buckley, P. J., and Ghauri, P. N. 2004. Globalization, economic geography, and the strategy of multinational enterprises. *Journal of International Business Studies*, 35: 81–98.

Buckley, P. J., and Strange, R. 2011. The governance of the multinational enterprise: Insights from internalization theory. *Journal of Management Studies*, 48: 460–470.

Buckley, P. J., Strange, R., Timmer, M. P., and de Vries, G. 2022. Rent appropriation in local value chains: The past, present, and future of intangible assets. *Global Strategy Journal*, 12(4): 679–696. March 31. https://doi.org/10.1002/gsj.1438.

Buttonwood. 2022. The inventory cycle returns. *The Economist*, June 4: 68.

Cantwell, J. 2013. Blurred boundaries between firms, and new boundaries within (large multinational) firms: the impact of decentralized networks for innovation. *Seoul Journal of Economics*, 26(1): 1–32.

Casson, M. 1987. *The Firm and the Market*. Oxford: Basil Blackwell.

Clark, D., and Bradsher, K. 2023. China scuttles a $5.4 billion microchip deal led by US giant Intel. *New York Times*, August 16. www.nytimes.com/2023/08/16/business/intel-tower-semiconductor-china.html?smid=em-share.

Dierickx, I., and Cool, K. 1989. Asset stock accumulation and sustainability of competitive advantage. *Management Science*, 35: 1504–1511.

Fukuyama, F. 1992. *The End of History and the Last Man*. New York: The Free Press.

Gereffi, G., Humphrey, J., and Sturgeon, T. 2005. The governance of global value chains. *Review of International Political Economy*, 12: 78–104.

Ghoshal, S. and Nohria, N. 1989. Internal differentiation within multinational corporations. *Strategic Management Journal*, 10: 323–337.

Granovetter, M. 1985. Economic action, social structure, and embeddedness. *American Journal of Sociology*, 91: 481–510.

Immelt, J., Govindarajan, V., and Trimble, C. 2009. How GE is disrupting itself. *Harvard Business Review*, 87(10): 56–65.

Koza, Mitchell P., and Lewin, A. 1996. *How to Manage in Times of Disorder*. Mastering Strategy Series (November 22, 1999). London: Financial Times .

Koza, Mitchell P., and Lewin, A. 1998. The coevolution of strategic alliances. *Organization Science*, 9(3): 255–264.

Koza, M. P., Tallman, S., and Ataay, A. 2011. The strategic assembly of global firms: A micro-structural analysis of local learning and global adaptation. *Global Strategy Journal*, 1(1): 27–46.

Lewin, A., and Volberda, H. 1999. Prolegomena on coevolution: A framework for research on strategy and new organizational firms. *Organization Science*, 10(5): 519–534.

McDermott, G., Mudambi, R., and Parente, R. 2013. Strategic modularity and the architecture of the multinational firm. *Global Strategy Journal*, 3: 1–7.

Mudambi, R. 2007. Offshoring: Economic geography and the multinational firm. *Journal of International Business Studies*, 38 (1): 206.

Mudambi, R. 2008. Location, control, and innovation in knowledge-intensive industries. *Journal of Economic Geography*, 8: 699–725.

Narula, R. and Dunning, J. H. 2010. Multinational enterprises, development and globalization: Some clarifications and a research agenda. *Oxford Development Studies*, 38(3): 263–287.

Petricevic, O., and Teece, D. J. 2019. The structural reshaping of globalization: Implications for strategic sectors, profiting from innovation, and the multinational enterprise. *Journal of International Business Studies*, 50: 1487–1512.

Prahalad, C. K., and Hamel, G. 1985. The core competence of the corporation. *Harvard Business Review*, 68/3: 79–91.

Rugman, A. M. 2005. *The Regional Multinationals*. Cambridge: Cambridge University Press.

Rugman, A. M., and D'Cruz, J. 1997. The theory of the flagship firm. *European Management Journal*, 15: 403–412.

Rumelt, R. P. 1974. *Strategy, Structure, and Economic Performance*. Boston: Division of Research, Graduate School of Business Administration, Harvard University.

Science Po. 2018. Multinational corporations. *World Atlas of Global Issues*, https://espace-mondial-atlas.sciencespo.fr/en/topic-strategies-of-trans national-actors/article-3A11-EN-multinational-corporations.html#.

Sturgeon, T. 2002. Modular production networks: A new American model of industrial organization. *Industrial and Corporate Change*, 11: 451–496.

Swanson, A. 2023. As ties to China turn toxic, even Chinese companies are breaking them. *New York Times*, June 15. www.nytimes.com/2023/06/15/business/economy/china-business-tiktok-shein.html?smid=em-share.

Tallman, S., and Koza, M. P. 2010. Keeping the global in mind: The evolution of headquarters in global multi-business firms. *Management International Review*, 50: 433–448.

Tallman, S. , and Koza, M. P. 2016. Strategic animation and emergent processes: Managing for efficiency and innovation in globally networked organizations. In T. Ambos, B. Ambos, and J. Birkinshaw, eds., *Perspectives on Headquarters-Subsidiary Relationships in the Contemporary MNC*, Research in Global Strategic Management, Vol. 17: 59–85. Bingley: Emerald.

Tallman, S. , and Koza, M. P. 2024. Reflections on global strategy in a turbulent world. In A. Hawk, M. Larsen, M. Leiblein, and J. Reuer, eds., *Strategy in a Turbulent Era*, pp. 2–17. Cheltenham: Edward Elgar.

Tallman, S., and Pedersen, T. 2015. What is international strategy research and what is not? *Global Strategy Journal*, 5: 273–277.

The Economist. 2022. Zero options, December 3: 19–22.

The Economist. 2023a. America's new best friend. June 17: 9.

The Economist. 2023b. BritGP. June 17: 10.

The Economist. 2023c. Schumpeter: Ford's focus. June 17: 58.

The Economist. 2023d. Spooked. June 17: 52–53.

The Economist. 2023e. The dragon shows its claws. July 29: 45–46.

The Economist. 2023f. Rising tiger, hidden dragon. August 12: 57–58.

Yen, B. 2016. *Uniqlo: A Supply Chain Going Global*. Hong Kong: University of Hong Kong Case Research Center.

Zenger, T. R., and Hesterly, W. S. 1997. The disaggregation of corporations: Selective intervention, high-powered incentives, and molecular units. *Organization Science*, 8/3: 209–222.

Acknowledgments

From Stephen B. Tallman:

For Marcia and Tess
For your support

From Mitchell P. Koza:

For Antoinette, Maxine, Leo, and Calvin,
Without whom this would not have been possible

And for

Charles E. Bidwell,
Without whom this would not have been necessary

Cambridge Elements ≡

Business Strategy

J.-C. Spender

Kozminski University

J.-C. Spender is a research Professor, Kozminski University. He has been active in the business strategy field since 1971 and is the author or co-author of 7 books and numerous papers. His principal academic interest is in knowledge-based theories of the private sector firm, and managing them.

About the Series

Business strategy's reach is vast, and important too since wherever there is business activity there is strategizing. As a field, strategy has a long history from medieval and colonial times to today's developed and developing economies. This series offers a place for interesting and illuminating research including industry and corporate studies, strategizing in service industries, the arts, the public sector, and the new forms of Internet-based commerce. It also covers today's expanding gamut of analytic techniques.

Cambridge Elements $\equiv$

Business Strategy

Elements in the Series

Printed in the United States
by Baker & Taylor Publisher Services